TIPS ON
TRAINING

insurance

Lorem ipsum dolor sit amet, consectetur adipscing elit, sed diam nonumy eirmod tempor incidunt ut labore et dolore magna aliquam erat volupat. Ut enim ad minimim veniami quis nostrud exercitation ullamcorpus suscipit laboris nisi ut aliquid ex ea commodo consequat. Duis autem vel eum irure dolor in reprehenderit in voluptate velit esse molestaie son consequat, vel illum dolore eu fugiat nulla pariatur. At vero eos et accusam et justo odio dignissim qui blandit praesent luptatum delenit aigue duos dolor et molestais exceptur sint occaecat cupidat non provident, simil tempor sunt in culpa qui officia deserunt mollit anim id est laborum et dolor fugai. Et harumd dereud facilis est er expedit distinct. Nam liber te conscient to factor tum poen legum odioque civiuda et tam. Neque pecun modut est neque nonor et imper ned libidig met, consectetur adipiscing elit, sed ut labore et dolore magna aliquam est er expedit distinct. Nam liber te conscient to factor tum poen legum odioque civiuda et tam. Neque pecun modut est neque nonor et imper ned libidig met, consectetur adipiscing elit, sed ut labore et dolore magna aliquam. Ut enim ad minima veniami, quis nostrud exercitation ullam corporis suscipit laboriosam, nisi ut aliquid ex ea commodi consequatur. Quis autem vel eum irure reprehenderit qui in ea voluptate velit esse quam nihil molestiae consequatur, vel illum qui dolorem eum fugiat quo voluptas nulla pariatur. At vero eos et accusam et justo odio dignissim qui blandit praesent luptatum delenit aigue duos dolor et molestais exceptur sint occaecat cupidat non provident, simil tempor sunt in culpa qui officia deserunt mollit anim id

TIPS ON TRAINING

Collaborated by the
Athletic Training Council
Editorial Committee

A structure of the
National Association
for Girls and
Women in Sport

an association of
The American Alliance for
Health, Physical Education,
Recreation and Dance

Copyright © 1983

The American Alliance for
Health, Physical Education,
Recreation and Dance
1900 Association Drive
Reston, Virginia 22091
ISBN 0-88314-231-7

Purposes of the American Alliance For Health, Physical Education, Recreation and Dance

The American Alliance is an educational organization, structured for the purposes of supporting, encouraging, and providing assistance to member groups and their personnel throughout the nation as they seek to initiate, develop, and conduct programs in health, leisure, and movement-related activities for the enrichment of human life.

Alliance objectives include:

1. Professional growth and development—to support, encourage, and provide guidance in the development and conduct of programs in health, leisure, and movement-related activities which are based on the needs, interests, and inherent capacities of the individual in today's society.

2. Communication—to facilitate public and professional understanding and appreciation of the importance and value of health, leisure, and movement-related activities as they contribute toward human well-being.

3. Research—to encourage and facilitate research which will enrich the depth and scope of health, leisure, and movement-related activities; and to disseminate the findings to the profession and other interested and concerned publics.

4. Standards and guidelines—to further the continuous development and evaluation of standards within the profession for personnel and programs in health, leisure, and movement-related activities.

5. Public affairs—to coordinate and administer a planned program of professional, public, and governmental relations that will improve education in areas of health, leisure, and movement-related activities.

6. To conduct such other activities as shall be approved by the Board of Governors and the Alliance Assembly, provided that the Alliance shall not engage in any activity which would be inconsistent with the status of an educational and charitable organization as defined in Section 501(c) (3) of the Internal Revenue Code of 1954 or any successor provision thereto, and none of the said purposes shall at any time be deemed or construed to be purposes other than the public benefit purposes and objectives consistent with such educational and charitable status. *Bylaws, Article III*

Athletic Training Council
Editorial Committee

Table of Contents

Introduction

The services provided for athletic medical care are extremely varied in high schools and colleges, ranging from a tray of ice cubes reserved for injury care to a fully equipped training room with a complete staff. Indeed, in these days of fiscal conservatism, a full-time athletic trainer, especially at the high school level, is an unaffordable luxury. While some schools make an attempt to identify some health-related staff member to deal with athletic injuries, others rely solely on coaches to recognize and treat injuries. All of these individuals are capable of acting in this capacity, but certainly not without proper training, as is so often the case.

Contrary to common belief, a first aid kit and tape supply do not a trainer make. Many a coach will attest to the fact that nothing in the training kit helps when an athlete suffers a concussion, sustains a fracture, or tears a ligament. In these cases, the most valuable tools a trainer can utilize are standard equipment—the hands and brain. In the absence of a trainer, almost any staff member can act responsibly enough to deal with these circumstances if there is a basic knowledge of the injury and its care. The coach, a student trainer, the school nurse, a local emergency medical technician, or therapist are such persons. In the case of athletic injury, it isn't so much what you are, as what you know.

It is the purpose of this manual to provide tips on athletic training to ancillary personnel so that they may ensure proper care through recognition and referral. Perhaps the most important responsibility is to know one's limitations. This also applies to trainers, who serve to refer problems which go beyond the scope of their expertise.

For the school nurse, EMT, coach, or other person assigned to athletic medical care, there are a few basic requirements. There is no substitute for, nor excuse for not knowing cardiopulmonary resuscitation (CPR). CPR courses are taught by the American Red Cross, the American Heart Association, and many colleges. The cost is minimal when the value of a life saved is considered. The second requirement should be standard first aid, which is likewise taught locally by the American Red Cross or through a college. These short courses are successfully taught to individuals aged 13 and older, and their life-saving successes are well-documented. Everyone can learn, and indeed, should learn CPR, especially when assuming responsibility for the care of athletes.

Regardless of efforts to train ancillary personnel for this role, the true answer to the problem is the availability of a certified athletic trainer. Few people realize the educational background of these professionals who are required to meet rigorous standards set by the National Athletic Trainers Association. Most athletic trainers acquire a B.S. degree in physical education, with emphasis in areas related to sports medicine such as anatomy, physiology, nutrition, kinesiology, exercise physiology, psychology, therapeutic exercise, evaluation, and of course, first aid. They are required to serve 800 hours (curriculum) to 1800 hours (apprentice) under the supervision of a certified athletic trainer in a practical setting. Before the national organization will certify candidates, they must prove competency in a variety of areas, through a thorough written and practical examination.

First and foremost, the athletic trainer is concerned with minimizing the inherent risk of sports. Responsibilities, thus, include first aid, evaluation, treatment and rehabilitation, pre-season screening, preventative taping and wrapping, assistance to the coach in developing conditioning programs, and education of coaches and athletes in areas of common concern such as nutrition and dieting. Prevention of injuries has been widely recognized as a primary concern, often accounting for 40–60% of the trainers' activities.

It has been said that the trainer is always the first to arrive to school and the last to leave, and this is not surprising when one considers his/her duties before, during, and after practice. Multiply these responsibilities times the numbers of teams practicing, and the demands on a trainer's time can be understood. Trainers are most energetic, often working 60–80 hours per week to accomodate the needs of athletes.

The major differences between an ancillary athletic care person and an athletic trainer are availability, scope of expertise, and prevention-orientation. It is most difficult to prove that preventative measures work; however, there are a few examples which illustrate quite clearly the merit of such efforts. A few years ago, some athletic trainers who studied the mechanism of football fatalities and neck fractures, discovered that spear-tackling was usually involved. Eventually this resulted in a rule change outlawing the technique, followed by a subsequent drop in the casualty rate. Likewise, trainers have also prevented muscle strains and joint sprains through enforcement of stretching and strengthening exercises prescribed for susceptible individuals. Ensuring health in this manner surely enriches the athletic experience for participants, and helps improve the quality of life through education about proper injury care and prevention.

The core of any injury prevention program is the pre-season physical examination, which should be required of all participants. While a routine physical exam may suffice for a sedentary or moderately active person, it will not suffice as a means of determining an athlete's participation fitness. In these days of increasing liability concerns, the pre-season physical exam has been recognized as a most important means of protecting both the individual and the institution. Though other health care persons may lend assistance, a medical doctor should direct and perform the major components of the pre-participation medical exam. The following screening examinations should be minimal requirements of the physical: medical history; height and weight; visual acuity; urinalysis; hemoglobin; sickle cell; menstrual history; orthopedic; blood pressure; pulse; general physical condition; flexibility; strength.

The medical history is an important source of information for the coach, trainer, and physician. It should identify non-sport related illnesses and injuries, as well as those commonly associated with athletics. Insurance information should be included on this form to expedite proper hospital care in the event of serious injury. The NAGWS Athletic Training Council has developed a medical history questionnaire specifically for women athletes and this is available to you at no charge (see Chapter 10).

The extent to which a coach utilizes valuable information gathered during the physical exam can certainly affect injury rate. If the predisposing factors to injury can be identified, the deficiency can be corrected. Thus the physical exam must include tests designed to identify deficiencies in joint stability, strength, and flexibility, factors which are related to injury. Identification of these factors is an injury *prediction* system. Coupled with specific remedial exercises, it can be an effective injury *prevention* system.

Because this type of detailed pre-participation screening is the exception to the rule, the athletes and administrators will have to be "sold" on its importance. Providing a comprehensive athletic screening is like buying injury protection insurance. Try it, and observe the results. Chances are that you can't afford *not* to maintain a screening program. The price paid out in terms of sidelined athletes just doesn't seem worth it.

Certainly there are some injuries that simply cannot be prevented. When a 130-pound baserunner collides with a 100-pound catcher blocking home plate, anything can happen. As the following chapters are read, note the emphasis on ensuring proper health care for the student athlete. The cornerstone of good health care is prevention; the rest lies in one's ability to recognize injury, perform athletic training skills within limitations, and refer athletes to medical professionals when necessary.

Planning a High School Athletic Training Program

Stanley Nakahara, A.T.C., M.S.

Finding an Appropriate Facility

An athletic training program can be a very valuable asset to the high school athletic program. The person who has been assigned the responsibility of starting an athletic training program must secure the use of a room. Preferably, the room should be in the locker room in a location that is accessible to all athletes, both boys and girls. If accessibility is a problem, it may be located outside the gym area. In securing this room, however, consideration should also be given to access to water, drains, ventilation, and electricity.[1]

The size of the training room is dependent on the number of students it is to serve and whether or not a certified athletic trainer is to utilize the facility. It should serve all students in the school, not only the boys and girls participating in the interscholastic sports program, but also those in the intramural and recreational programs and the physical education classes. Therefore, the size of the school and the extent of the program will determine the space required.[2]

The minimum space needed for an adequately equipped training room is an area 15 feet by 20 feet (300 square feet). This is the minimum area required for one taping table, one treatment table, a sink with some counter space, and basic training room equipment such as a refrigerator or ice machine and a whirlpool.[3]

A rough estimate of the area required can be made by determining how many treatment and taping tables are needed to adequately serve the students. Approximately 100 square feet of space is needed for each table. This estimate includes the table or bench size, the working area around the table, and the associated counter and storage space.[4] About 20 athletes can be accommodated per table on any given day prior to a practice or contest. By dividing the number of students that the area is to serve during the peak load by 20, then multiplying that number by 100, the approximate number of square feet needed for the training room can be determined.[5] The floor of the training room should be constructed of concrete and covered with vinyl tile or one of the new synthetic non-slip resin floor coatings that can be readily cleaned. The training room collects dirt and debris carried in from various activity areas, yet it must be kept clean and sanitary. These synthetic resin materials are suitable for all floors including those in wet areas. They are not slippery and can be readily hosed off. The material should be applied about 4 inches up the side of the wall.[6]

The hydrotherapy equipment (the refrigerator, the ice machine, and the whirlpool) should be installed in an area separate from the other training room equipment. As a result of space limitations, the equipment may be placed in one corner of the room. A curb to separate this hydrotherapy area from the rest of the training room is not necessary if the floor is sloped and if the drainage is adequate. The floor of the hydrotherapy area should have a slope of approximately 1% and there should be more than one drain. This slope accommodates drainage which creates an area that is easier to clean and safe.[7]

[1]Klafs, C. E., and Arnheim, D. D. *Modern Principles of Athletic Training*. St. Louis, MO: C. V. Mosby Company, 1981.
[2]Ibid., 1981.
[3]Penman, K. A., et al. "Training Rooms Aren't Just for Colleges." *Athletic Purchasing and Facilities* 6 (9): 34–7.
[4]Ibid., 1981, pp. 34–7.
[5]Ibid., 1981, pp. 34–7.
[6]Ibid., 1981, pp. 34–7.
[7]Ibid., 1981, pp. 34–7.

Construction of this hydrotherapy area is a major task because existing plumbing may need to be altered to provide an adequate number of water outlets and drains. In fact, it is necessary to anticipate the number of whirlpools that may ultimately be required so that the rough plumbing can be installed when the room is being redone or constructed.

If the room is being redone, outside windows should be eliminated if possible. If a new room is being constructed and windows are required, they should be placed above the hydrotherapy area at least 7 feet from the floor. In a room where there are separate areas, indoor windows may be necessary for proper supervision of the entire room. Doors should be sufficiently wide to maneuver a stretcher or gurney in and out of the training room. A Dutch door is ideal to prevent undue traffic in the training room. The walls should be covered with a glossy paint which permits easy cleaning. A light color such as light green or white makes the room appear more "antiseptic"; however, any color is suitable if it has good reflection characteristics. The walls around the hydrotherapy area should be ceramic tile or a synthetic resinous material similar to the floor surface. A counter with cabinets and a sink should be installed along one wall in the main training room area. The cabinets should lock and the sink should have hot and cold running water. A soap dispenser and a paper towel holder should be placed above the sink. Cupboards with lockable sliding doors should be securely attached to the wall above the counter. A bulletin board should be attached near the door. A few ankle wrap rollers should be installed just outside the door.[8]

The electrical features of the training room should include florescent lighting which is very energy-efficient. Such lighting illuminates between 50 to 60 foot candles. The electrical outlets should all be grounded and a reset switch should be included in each of the outlets in the hydrotherapy area. The outlets in the entire room should be approximately 4 feet apart and 4 feet from the floor.[9]

The temperature desired for the most efficiency in the training room should be approximately 76–78°. The warmer temperature is required because athletes are usually sparsely dressed while in the room.[10]

Setting up a Training Room

Once the room has been secured and modified, or built, the individual must equip it with some basic equipment and supplies. The training room should have a desk, a chair, and a file if a designated individual is assigned to supervise the area. (Hopefully, the individual is a certified athletic trainer.) An accessible telephone with an outside line is an absolute necessity for emergency calls. The most important piece of athletic training equipment is a refrigerator or an ice machine. The refrigerator must be capable of making large quantities of ice. In larger training rooms, a separate ice machine may be necessary to supply the demand.[11]

Treatment tables should be approximately 30 inches high, 2 feet wide, and 6 to 7 feet long. They should be covered by a foam pad and a synthetic plastic cover of some type for ease in cleaning. Taping tables are approximately half the length of a treatment table. The two types of tables can be built from either wood or metal in various ways. Every trainer usually has a preference for material and a method of construction, but the budget may be an important factor to consider. Construction of such tables is an ideal project for students in the advanced wood and metal shop classes at the school.[12]

Two different size whirlpools should be considered for the hydrotherapy areas—the full body size and the smaller extremity size. If possible, at least one of each size should be installed to meet the various demands and also to conserve energy. In some high schools there may be a corrective or adaptive physical education room adjacent to the training room. Students in the corrective or adapted program might also use the whirlpool(s) providing such a treatment is prescribed by the attending physician.

Lockable cupboards are necessary to store supplies used in the training room. Such supplies include the basic items used in the first aid care and follow-up treatment of athletic injuries. Items such as tape, ankle wraps, elastic bandages, gauze pads, gauze rolls, bandaids, moleskin, adhesive foam, aluminum finger splints, slings, tape adherent, tape remover, external analgesics of various strengths, first aid solutions, ointments and creams, paper cups, and plastic bags may be stored on the shelves in the cupboard. Special "instruments" such as a thermometer, blood pressure cuff, stethoscope, and possibly an ophthalmoscope/oto-

[8]Ibid., 1981, pp. 34–7.
[9]Ibid., 1981, pp. 34–7.
[10]Ibid., 1981, pp. 34–7.
[11]Ibid., 1981, pp. 34–7.
[12]Ibid., 1981, pp. 34–7.

scope, should be secured in a separate area of the cupboard. Dressing jars containing gauze pads, cotton-tipped applicators, cotton balls, and tongue depressors should be readily available on the counter top but locked up at the end of the day. The same applies to scissors, tape cutters, and hair clippers; otherwise, they have a tendency to disappear. Larger items such as blankets, pillows, and assorted materials used for protective padding should be stored on separate shelving. Crutches and spine boards can be hung on wall hooks and ice chests can be stacked in the hydrotherapy area.[13]

Since these supplies often have to be purchased on bid in large quantities, a storage closet or room should be secured. Bulk supplies such as cases of tape, large splints, and other large items can be stored in this closet or room. The storage space should be clean, cool, and dry. It should also be secured by a lock to ensure not only safety but the availability of supplies when needed.

Finances and Budgeting

Besides acquiring a facility, an important facet of the athletic training program is how to finance the facility. Some school districts specify funds in the school's athletic budget to supply and equip a training room. Many times, however, the training room budget is neglected to the point to which it is inadequate. If this is the case, as the individual who cares for the welfare of all the participants, support may be gained from parents, coaches, players, and administrators. Demonstrate to them a very definite need to upgrade the athletic training program.

One of the popular ways of acquiring money is fund-raising. Hold jog-a-thons, car washes, sell candy or school spirit items, and run concession stands at home games. Acquire a drink machine to sell drinks to the students. The money from these fund-raisers and concessions can then be used to equip the training room. Another way to finance the training room is to coordinate the special education budget for remedial and/or adapted physical education. Sometimes equipment can be bought which could be used in this special program as well as the athletic training program.

In determining a budget, be aware of the number of sport participants. One person should order all the training supplies and be responsible for distribution of the items. This will help to eliminate waste and economize the use of all supplies. Inventory will then be easier and so will the ordering of supplies for the following year.

When what is needed for ordering is determined, shop around at different suppliers to price the supplies. Specify exactly what is needed and do not accept any substitutes.

In setting up a training room, the initial cost is likely to be high because equipment as well as supplies must be ordered. As the program continues, the non-reuseable items are the only items that must be reordered on a yearly basis, unless the facility expands.

The training facility needs to be maintained yearly by student trainers. They can be recruited from the physical education classes or the interscholastic teams. Once a training facility is acquired, continually search for new and better ways to help maintain a high quality of professionalism and service in the facility. This training room can be an integral part of an outstanding interscholastic athletic program.

---

[13]Ibid, 1981, pp. 34–7.

Basic Athletic Injury Care

2

Katie Heffelfinger, A.T.C.

Acute traumatic injuries in athletics pose a unique problem for the trainer, team physician, coach, and the athlete. It is the responsibility of the medical support personnel and the coach working together to resolve these problems, along with the total cooperation of the injured athlete, which is essential, to get the individual safely back into the competitive environment as soon as possible.

It is imperative that the coach, trainer, and team physician have a methodical procedure to follow when evaluating athletic injuries to ensure the safety and well-being of the athlete.

The first step in injury evaluation should be to get a history of the incident. How did the injury occur? Did it seem mild or severe? Did the athlete feel or hear a noise? All of these questions and more will give vital clues to the nature of the injury.

The next step should be a physical examination of the injured area. The examiner should *observe*, noting the general appearance at the site of the injury. He/she should look for swelling, deformity, damage to the skin, and bruising. Next, *palpitation* of the area should be done to feel any abnormalities or irregularities that may be present. *Functional testing* of the injured area can determine the pain, loss of function, and instability on both active and passive ranges of motion; however, such tests should only be carried out by a trainer, paramedic, or physician. As a coach, the range of motion of the injured part can be checked by asking the athlete to move that part through its pain-free range. With musculoskeletal injuries, an *x-ray examination* may be ordered by the attending physician to provide additional insight into the extent of injury.

Immediate injury management consists of five primary procedures: (1) application of ice; (2) compression; (3) elevation; (4) immobilization; (5) controlled rest.

The benefits derived from immediate application of ice to traumatic injuries such as a sprain, strain, fracture, contusion, and dislocation cannot be overemphasized. Cold causes vasoconstriction (a decrease in the size of the blood vessel), decreases swelling in the surrounding tissues, reduces muscle spasticity and also reduces the sensation of pain. The initial ice treatment should be in the form of an ice slush bath, shaved ice pack, or cold whirlpool and should last 20-30 minutes. Ice therapy should be continued for approximately 15-20 minutes every hour for the next 48-72 hours, depending on the severity of the injury, or until swelling and hemorrhaging have been completely controlled.

Compression is the second essential when treating acute athletic injuries. Compression in the form of an elastic bandage, foam or felt padding, athletic tape, or a combination of all three help to reduce the potential for swelling to the injured joint or soft tissue area. (See Figure 1.) It is of great importance that the compression be applied firmly but not so tight as to cut off blood circulation to the injury site. During the initial ice application, compression should be applied by wrapping the involved area with an elastic bandage. (See Figure 2.) The bandage should be wet to help conduct the coldness to the tissue. Compression should be maintained after the ice therapy with a dry elastic bandage and/or athletic tape.

Elevation, the third part of the standard first aid procedure (I.C.E.) requires that the injured joint or limb be raised slightly above the horizontal plane to aid in the control of or prevention of swelling. (See Figure 3.) However, any suspected fracture should first be temporarily splinted. The involved part

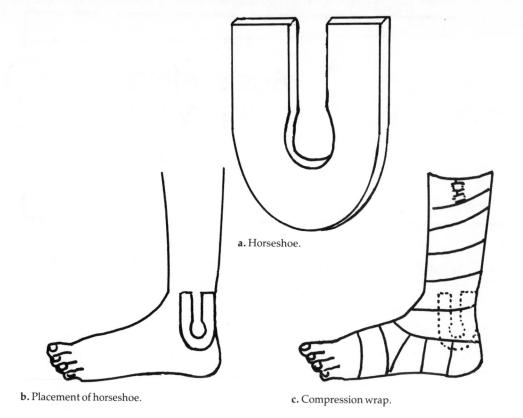

a. Horseshoe.

b. Placement of horseshoe.

c. Compression wrap.

Figure 1. Horseshoe and compression wrap.

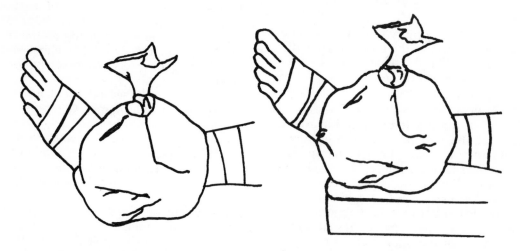

Figure 2. Ice pack on injury.

Figure 3. Elevation of injury.

should be elevated whenever possible during the initial injury and recovery stages.

Severe injuries such as fractures, dislocations, and second or third degree sprains and strains require temporary splinting or immobilization to prevent further tissue trauma and to control pain. Such injuries will undoubtedly require more permanent immobilization in the form of a rigid splint, cast, or some type of tape strapping to en-

courage and expedite the healing process. When needed, immobilization is prescribed by the team physician or trainer.

The final step to be considered in the management of athletic injuries is controlled rest. This may be the most difficult aspect of injury management for the athlete as well as the coach. It is the coach's responsibility to give total support to the team physician or trainer during the duration of the recommended rest period. Rest or inactivity in the mind of the athlete is taboo. Therefore, the reasons for the rest must be thoroughly explained to the athlete; his or her total cooperation and dedication is essential to achieve the desired results. Controlled rest will usually include some type of daily therapy such as therapeutic rehabilitation exercises along with modality treatments.

The appropriate initial management of the athletic injury may make the difference in the athlete being able to return to action in a matter of minutes or days as opposed to several weeks of inactivity due to poor management procedures.

Types of Injuries

Sprains

A sprain is one of the most common disabling injuries seen in athletics. It is a first degree stretching, a second degree partial tearing, or a third degree complete tearing (rupture) of the ligamentous structures surrounding the joint. Sprains are usually caused by traumatic twisting of the joint resulting in over-stretching or tearing of one or more ligaments. Ligaments are inelastic fibrous bands that join one bone to another, thus forming a joint. These bands are designed to prevent abnormal range of motion of the joint while permitting normal functional motion. Most sprains are seen in the ankle, knee, and shoulder joints.

In the first degree sprain, there is little functional loss with only a few ligamentous fibers involved in the over-stretching process. The signs to look for will include: point tenderness; a small amount of swelling; discoloration (in some cases). Treatment should include ice, compression, and elevation (I.C.E.), and maintenance of range of motion as well as strengthening exercises.

The second degree sprain is a more serious ligamentous injury resulting in a partial tearing of the ligament fibers. There will be local tenderness, moderate swelling, hemorrhaging, and some loss of function. The standard I.C.E. procedure is appropriate first aid treatment. Usually the team physician will also recommend immobilization and possibly surgery to repair the damage to the joint structure.

The third degree sprain is a complete rupture of one or more of the stabilizing ligaments. The symptoms are more extreme than those associated with the second degree. Surgery is usually required to restore joint stability and function.

Strains

Strain refers to the injury that involves the muscle tendon unit. The strain may range from a minute separation of fibers caused by over-stretching or a forceful contraction, to a complete separation or rupture somewhere along the unit. A strain can be very painful and debilitating depending on severity and location. The most common strains seen in athletics include those of the hamstrings, quadriceps, groin area, low back, and biceps.

The first degree strain will produce no apparent disruption of the musculotendinous unit but there will be discomfort on function, low grade inflammation, and some muscle spasticity. Immediate treatment should include I.C.E. with slight stretching of the involved muscle but only to the point where discomfort is first felt. After ice therapy, apply a dry elastic bandage to maintain compression on the area. Care should be taken to prevent further damage to the area. Rehabilitation involves gradual strengthening and stretching of the injured muscle. The athlete should not return to activity until both range of motion and strength are normal and pain-free.

When the second degree strain occurs there is actual damage due to partial tearing of the muscle, tendon, or the attachment which will cause definite loss of normal function and pain. The athlete will demonstrate pain upon contraction of the affected area; there will be point tenderness, swelling, the possibility of hemorrhaging, muscle spasticity, and loss of strength. Treatment will include immediate application of I.C.E. plus stretching to the point of discomfort, and controlled rest. Ice therapy must be continued until swelling is controlled, 48–72 hours later. Ice treatment should be continued or heat application begun. When pain is absent, a slow cautious strengthening and stretching program should be begun. Protection in the form of a compression wrap and a thorough daily warmup stretching routine will be necessary to prevent re-injury when the athlete returns to action.

The third degree strain is the most serious because it involves a separation or rupture of the muscle through its belly, its musculotendinous junction or its tendinous attachment. The actual separation may be palpated; at other times only the bunching up of muscle fibers can be felt. There will be pain at the site of the injury, swelling, lack of integrity of the musculotendinous unit, spasticity of the muscle fibers, and hemorrhaging. Usually surgery, immobilization, and rest are required for the best recovery.

The best treatment for strains is prevention. Care must be taken to ensure that the athlete has knowledge of the importance of warm-up and stretching techniques, and adequate time to perform them.

Dislocations

Dislocations and subluxations (partial dislocations) of the joint present a special problem in terms of handicapping the athlete. They primarily result from forces that cause the joint articulation to go beyond its normal anatomical range of motion. When subluxation occurs, there is partial separation between the two articulating bones causing damage to the surrounding soft tissue and joint capsule. A dislocation occurs when the two articulating bones are forced completely apart, usually causing moderate to severe damage to the surrounding soft tissues and joint capsule.

The majority of serious dislocations and subluxations occur in the shoulder joint of the athlete. Finger, toe, and patellar (kneecap) dislocations are also common.

There are three major factors to be considered when evaluating a possible dislocation:

- visual deformity is almost always present or deformity can be felt when palpated unless the joint has spontaneously reduced (gone back into place);
- after a severe blow or fall, if the joint has been dislocated, the athlete is unable to move that joint;
- there will be immediate pain and swelling.

Treatment for the dislocation and subluxation should be immediate ice application and stabilization of the affected joint. It is imperative that medical attention be immediately secured to determine the extent of damage to the joint capsule, muscles, tendons, and ligaments. All dislocations and subluxations should be x-rayed to make sure there have been no bone fragments pulled away at the tendon and ligament attachments. Since the stabilizing structures of the joint have been seriously traumatized, the joint should be immobilized for a period of one to six weeks. If possible, during the first 48-72 hours, ice should be applied to reduce pain, swelling, and muscle spasm. The immobilization period should be followed by an extensive program to regain normal range of motion of the involved and surrounding joints and strength of the surrounding musculature.

Unfortunately even with complete rehabilitation of the injury, once an athlete suffers a dislocation, there is greater chance for recurrence due to a weakness in the surrounding stabilizing structure.

Fractures

Although not seen as often in athletics as sprains and strains are, the coach and trainer should be prepared to handle a fracture emergency. A fracture is defined as an interruption in the continuity of a bone (a break in the bone). The break may be partial or complete. There are two types of fractures: a closed (simple) fracture; an open (compound) fracture, one in which one or both ends of the broken bone extends through the outer skin. Fractures should be suspected in any musculoskeletal injury and therefore, an x-ray is often warranted. An x-ray is the only positive way to determine the possibility of a fracture.

The signs and symptoms indicating a fracture are: specific pain (point tenderness) at the area of the break; general tenderness around the area; immediate swelling; visual or palpable deformity; discoloration. The coach, trainer, or team physician should also be aware of the history of the injury—a direct blow, hard fall, or a twisting type of injury caused by a great amount of force. In addition, the athlete may have heard or felt the bone snap.

Immediate treatment should include the application of ice, temporary splinting, elevation, and treatment for shock followed by referral to a physician for examination, x-ray, and casting. The healing process may take six to eight weeks or more.

The optimal treatment of fracture depends upon the prompt and definitive care given immediately at the time and site of the injury. Poor handling of a fracture may cause additional involvement of surrounding muscles, nerves, blood vessels, or internal organs.

Another type of injury frequently seen in athletics is the stress fracture. This is a hairline fracture of the bone that does not go through the entire bone. This type of injury may be deceptive because there is usually no history of injury. X-rays may be negative in the early stages and yet the symptoms persist. Stress fractures are found mostly in the metatarsal area (forefoot) and the lower half of the fibula due to the constant stress and pounding these areas absorb during athletic endeavors.

The signs of a stress fracture are persistent point tenderness and small amounts of swelling. The stress fracture may not be seen in the early x-ray and so if suspected, the area should be x-rayed every week to witness the formation of callous build-up as the natural healing process takes over.

Once it has been determined that a stress fracture exists, care should be taken to pad and protect the area and a period of rest may be indicated by the team physician. Ice is initially indicated to reduce inflammation and later heat may be applied to increase circulation to the area.

Contusion

A contusion may be defined as a direct blow to an area of the body causing bruising of the skin and underlying muscle due to capillary rupture and infiltrative bleeding. The result is a tender localized area of swelling and discoloration with possible muscle spasm commonly referred to as a bruise. If the blow is severe enough or repeated frequently to the same area, immature bone cells from the underlying bone may be released into the muscle fibers. Upon maturity, many months later, a bone has developed within the muscle, a condition known as myositis ossificans.

The treatment of a contusion consists of the standard I.C.E. procedure in the initial stages (the first 48–72 hours), immobilization in severe cases, and at all times, protection to prevent further injury or re-injury.

If the injury is minor and there is very little bleeding or swelling that does not interfere with functional use of the part, little treatment may be required after the initial I.C.E. However, if there is extensive bleeding and inflammation, the I.C.E. procedure should be prolonged until swelling is completely controlled; activity may have to be limited during this period. Local heat may be applied to encourage healing and help dissipate the remaining waste products once swelling is controlled.

Rehabilitation of the contusion injury should begin slowly and be within the limits of pain. It should include active stretching and range of motion and strengthening exercises. Some kind of pad should be made to protect the area against further trauma.

Open Wounds

Open wounds can be easily and safely handled by the athlete, coach, or trainer if a few general precautions are taken. The most serious problem facing any skin lesion is the possibility of infection. Even the most minor open wounds are subject to infection if not properly handled.

In general, all open wounds should be cleaned with soap and water to rid them of contamination. Then an antiseptic and a sterile dressing should be applied. Be sure the athlete has a current tetanus booster. It is effective for ten years but one should be administered if the athlete has not had a booster within five years of the date of the injury, that is, if tetanus is a distinct threat.

Abrasions

Abrasions are scraping injuries to the skin that may range from simple to extensive damage to the skin. Abrasions themselves are easily handled if the basic first aid measures to prevent infection are followed.

Lacerations

A laceration is a separation of the skin usually caused by a sharp object; the edge of the cut is usually jagged. Small lacerations can be treated by the coach or trainer. The bleeding is best stopped with direct pressure. The wound must be thoroughly cleaned with soap and water and an antiseptic and a sterile bandage applied. Most severe lacerations should be seen by a physician after initial first aid measures to control bleeding have been taken. The physician will then have the opportunity to clean the wound, apply steri-strips or sutures, if needed, and dress the wound.

Puncture Wounds

The puncture wound is not common in athletics but should be promptly and properly handled when it does occur. It is usually caused by a sharp object penetrating just into the skin or the underlying soft tissue. The chance of infection is great with the puncture wound. In most cases, there is very little bleeding which naturally cleanses the wound and the deep underlying portion of the wound may close over before it is examined, trapping in the contaminating bacteria and providing an ideal environment in which the anaerobic tetanus bacteria can multiply.

Treatment of the puncture wound, if minor, may only call for a complete cleaning of the wound with soap and water and observation of the wound as healing takes place to ensure that there is no infection developing (which is an important part of the standard care for any wound). The more serious puncture wound should only be protected from further contamination and seen immediately by a physician to determine the amount of damage to underlying tissues and to receive proper treatment. Do not clean the wound or remove any impaled object. If necessary, a tetanus booster will be given.

Blisters

Every athlete at one time or another will probably suffer from a blister. Because they are so common it is important that they are correctly treated to avoid any unnecessary discomfort or infection to the athlete. Poor management of a blister may cause an athlete to lose precious practice or game time.

Blisters are caused by friction from various sources, the most common being poor-fitting shoes and socks rubbing the skin, improperly applied athletic tape, and the wedging effect caused by callus build-up. These will cause the outer layers of the skin to separate from the underlying dermis where a pocket of fluid or blood will collect. Blisters are mostly seen on the backs of the heels, balls of the feet, on the toes, and palms of the hands.

The best treatment of blisters is prevention. This can easily be done by making sure the shoes and socks fit properly, the socks are clean, powder is put in the shoes and socks, callouses are kept shaved so they are flush with the skin, and a good tape adherent is used before applying athletic tape.

When blisters do occur, caution must be taken to prevent infection and to make the athlete as comfortable as possible. Anytime the skin is open, the chance of infection increases markedly. The intact blister can be protected from additional trauma with a felt donut. However, if the blister is torn, trim completely around the edge of the raised area with sterile scissors to remove the torn tissue. Make sure the trimmed edge is smooth. Clean the tender area with soap and water and then apply the donut. Place a small amount of petroleum jelly in the donut hole (antiseptic ointment or cream if the blister is open) and cover the donut with a sterile gauze pad. Tape the two securely in place. A small amount of petroleum jelly can be applied to the outer surface of the tape to lessen friction. Check the blister daily, especially one that has been trimmed, for signs of infection, and change the donut. When the new tissue under the raised skin is no longer tender, cut off the covering with sterile scissors. Continue to protect the area with a donut, petroleum jelly, and sterile gauze pad for the next few days. Thereafter, just apply the petroleum jelly as a precaution.

Splinting and Immobilization

Some type of splinting or immobilization should be applied to any musculoskeletal injury before the athlete is transported from the injury site. If the area of injury is not properly immobilized, further damage to underlying tissues, nerves, and blood vessels could ensue and shock could occur as a result of the trauma.

Splinting devices should always be accessible during athletic competition and practice sessions. The use of padded boards or airsplints is recommended. Always stabilize the joints above and below the site of the fracture.

Fractures of the ankle or lower leg require immobilization of the foot up to and including the knee. Any fracture involving the knee requires immobilization of the entire extremity. With involvement of the upper leg and/or hip, the splint must also extend upward along the trunk. Fractures of the hand, wrist, and lower arm require splinting in a position of forearm flexion and a sling. Fractures of the elbow and upper arm require straight arm immobilization while dislocations of the elbow are splinted in flexion, the position in which the injury was found. Shoulder injuries require that the shoulder joint be relaxed. This can best be accomplished by having the athlete hold the involved arm in a comfortable position while using an elastic bandage to secure it to the body. A general rule when immobilizing and splinting an injured limb is to splint the limb in the position in which it was found; hopefully this will be more comfortable to the athlete.

Injuries to the neck and spine in athletics pose a problem that should only be handled by those trained and qualified in such matters. When a neck or spine injury is suspected, the athlete should be immobilized and not moved until the help of emergency medical technicians, paramedics, or a physician is obtained.

The Unconscious Athlete

One of the most potentially serious situations faced by a coach or trainer is that of the unconscious athlete. This condition can be brought about by a blow to either the head or solar plexus or by general shock.

Figure 4. Taking the carotid pulse.

The following steps are suggested in the evaluation of the unconscious athlete:

1. Know the history of the injury either firsthand or by the accounts of those who witnessed the injury.
2. Assume there has been a neck or spine injury. Do not move the individual unless absolutely necessary and then only as a unit. Stabilize the head and neck at all times.
3. Quickly access the situation. Visually inspect the athlete and decide which part of the body was most affected by the injury. Check to see if breathing is normal and then check the carotid pulse. (See Figure 4.) If needed, begin artificial respiration or cardiopulmonary resuscitation. Otherwise progress with a thorough physical examination, beginning with an examination of the head. Determine first if there is bleeding or straw-colored fluid coming from the nose, ears, eyes, or mouth. Look for bumps, lacerations, or deformities that might indicate a skull fracture; next, move down the body and check for deformity.

If at all possible, the unconscious athlete should not be moved from the field until consciousness has been regained. The coach and trainer should avoid the use of ammonia caps to arouse the athlete when there is question of a neck or spinal cord injury. Once the athlete is coherent, the individual should be questioned as to pain, numbness, and tingling and tested for injury to the spinal cord and paralysis (sensation is felt; there is movement of fingers and toes).

All athletes suffering an injury causing unconsciousness should be removed from play and seen by a physician for a complete examination. The physician should be supplied with information about the circumstances of the injury and the length of time the athlete was unconscious.

Cardiopulmonary Resuscitation (CPR)

Trainers and coaches should have a working knowledge and be certified in the techniques of CPR. Classes are scheduled throughout the year by the American Red Cross or the American Heart Association. Hopefully, this knowledge will never be put to practical use.

The case of the athlete who has been injured so seriously that he/she is not breathing and the heart is not beating is a crisis that calls for immediate action. The purpose of CPR is to (1) establish an airway; (2) restore breathing; (3) restore circulation. The techniques are not difficult to learn and each coach and trainer should be encouraged to acquire these skills.

Treatment of Injuries 3

Toni Van DePutte, A.T.C.
and
Holly Wilson, A.T.C., Ph.D.

Since both cold and heat are used in the treatment of athletic injuries, the question of when to use what frequently arises. A brief summary of the physiological effects of these two physical agents may help to better understand the appropriate use of each.

Cold in any form causes vasoconstriction of the blood vessels in the area of application. The diameter of each vessel decreases in size, thus permitting less blood to flow through the area at a given time. Such a response may be helpful in the immediate care of a new injury to control swelling; however, in most instances, by the time the ice is applied the clotting mechanism has already sealed off the damaged blood vessels. What swelling results from the leaking of blood into the area has already occurred, but bleeding is not the only source of swelling. More important in treating the new injury is the fact that cold decreases the metabolic rate of the cells in the area being treated. Consequently, the cells do not need as much oxygen. At a time when the availability of oxygen is limited by trauma to its transport system, circulation, this response may actually prevent the death of cells by oxygen starvation. Tissue damage associated with an injury has two components: initial damage caused by the traumatic force; secondary damage from the lack of oxygen. Cut down the oxygen needs of the cells and tissue damage is not as great. Cold also has an anaesthetic effect, reducing pain but not entirely eliminating the sensation. The body's early warning system is still functioning. This anaesthetic effect is important in the immediate treatment of the injury when pain is intense and during the early stages of rehabilitation when working on range of motion. Finally, cold relieves muscle spasm. In many musculoskeletal injuries the body naturally attempts to splint the injury by tightening the muscles in the area.

The tight muscles must relax if rehabilitation is to progress. These effects, anaesthesia and reduction of muscle spasm, may last from several minutes to several hours following cold treatment. The cold actually interferes with the transmission of nerve impulses and such interference lasts a varying amount of time.

On the other hand, heat causes vasodilation, an increase in the diameter, of the blood vessels. Consequently more blood flows through the area at a given time. If heat is applied to the affected part immediately following an injury, swelling may increase as a result of the vasodilation and recovery would be delayed. However, vasodilation can be manipulated in treating the "older injury," one that is no longer swelling and has already passed through the inflammatory stage (heat, redness, pain, swelling, etc.). Such an injury is 48–72 hours old and into the repair and healing stage. The increased blood flow delivers the additional nutrients and oxygen required for repair and also carries away the metabolic byproducts as well as the debris remaining from the initial trauma. Heat causes an increase in the metabolism of the cells in the area of application, thus increasing their need for oxygen. If heat is immediately applied to a new injury, many cells would die from oxygen starvation because their needs could not be met by the impaired circulation. Heat also causes relaxation but the response usually lasts only as long as the treatment, i.e., once the treatment is terminated and the warm soothing sensation disappears, so does relaxation. Finally, heat relieves pain but that relief is not as enduring with cold application.

A simple test can determine when it is safe to apply heat. This test uses signs associated with the inflammatory response. With inflammation there is an increase in local tissue temperature at the injury site and the involved tissue is red in comparison to the surrounding tissue. As long as the involved tissue feels warmer or appears redder than the surrounding tissue or the corresponding part, heat should not be applied. The area is still inflamed and additional swelling remains a distinct possibility. Continue with the cold applications until there is no difference in skin temperature or color.

Both cold and heat must be cautiously used in the treatment of injuries. Although frostbite is rarely a problem in a controlled therapeutic setting, there are certain precautions that must be taken when cold is applied to the skin. Never apply cold to:

- an area that has been previously frostbitten;
- an individual suffering from Raynaud's Syndrome (sensitivity to the cold in which peripheral circulation is restricted by constriction of the blood vessels);
- an individual with a circulatory disturbance.

During the treatment, the individual may complain of extremely intense cold followed by a burning sensation which is short-lived and followed by a tingling, aching, stinging sensation and finally numbness. Although these are the same sensations experienced by the individual going into frostbite, there is one big difference. In frostbite, the skin turns white because blood flow is directed elsewhere to maintain the body's core temperature. In a controlled therapeutic setting, the skin color should remain a bright red during the cold application and for a short period of time thereafter. If the area being treated does turn white, remove the source of cold immediately.

There are more precautions associated with a heat treatment than with cold because burning of the tissue is always a distinct possibility. To limit the likelihood of burning someone, all heat applications should be warm and soothing to the individual. Make sure the individual understands this; some individuals may tolerate a little discomfort thinking if a little heat is good, more must be better. Always remember that tolerance to heat varies with each individual: usually those with darker complexions and darker hair color tolerate heat better than those with lighter coloring. Whenever heat is applied, the following precautions must be kept in mind. Never apply heat to:

- a new injury (one less than 48–72 hours old);
- an area where metal is embedded such as surgical screws, pins, and plates—metal attracts heat and could cause internal tissue burning;
- the eyes or genital area, both of which are sensitive to heat;
- an area where there is a circulatory disturbance such as a purplish-red swollen contusion;
- an area where there is no sensation because the individual cannot feel if the heat is burning the tissue.

Cold Therapy

Cold therapy (cryotherapy) can be applied in a number of ways—as an ice pack, ice slush, or ice massage. Each of these techniques will be discussed in detail; however, all these cryotherapy techniques are inexpensive, economical, easy to apply, relatively safe, easy to set up at home, and with little inconvenience.

Ice Pack

An ice pack can be applied to almost any area of the body with little difficulty. To make an ice pack, chips or cubes of ice are placed in a moist towel or a plastic bag. The pack is then placed on the traumatized area that has, hopefully, already been wrapped with a wet elastic bandage for compression. Both the pack and the compression bandage are wet to help conduct the cold more quickly to the part. Ice chips mold to the body part better than ice cubes but do not last as long.

The pack should remain in place for up to 30 minutes. In review of cryotherapy literature, there is some controversy concerning the amount of time cold should be applied immediately after an injury. There has been some confusion whether reflex dilation of the blood vessels actually takes place when a cold application is left on the skin too long. This reflex dilation is thought to be a safeguard against frostbite. Obviously, dilation of the blood vessels should be avoided in treating the new injury. Research has shown that such dilation occurs only in those areas of the body that are sensitive to the cold, i.e., the fingers, toes, nose, breasts, and genitalia. Consequently, it is safe to apply cold as long as 30 minutes and it is recommended that cryotherapy be repeated every hour and a half for the 30-minute time period. However, cold need not be applied to the new injury during the night as long as the involved part is elevated and a compression bandage remains in place. Adequate sleep is also an essential part of the healing process.

Although ice packs are extremely useful, good contact between the involved tissue and the pack may be limited by anatomical features. Consequently, cold packs may not be as effective a cooling agent as other forms of cryotherapy.

Ice Slush

Cooling is uniform in this form of cryotherapy because slush conforms to the bony anatomy. In fact, ice slush is ideal for treating the distal aspects of either extremity. Unfortunately in treating new injuries with this technique, the beneficial effects of compression and elevation on swelling must be sacrificed. In exchange, the deepest cold penetration of all cryotherapy is attained.

To set up an ice slush treatment, fill a large container with water and ice until the temperature reaches equilibrium between 55–65° F. Caution the athlete receiving the treatment that it is initially extremely painful, but the treatment time is not as long as with an ice pack. Treatment is terminated when the affected part is numb, usually from 5–10 minutes.

This treatment is especially desired when the athlete is attempting to regain range of motion. The buoyancy of the water and the anaesthetic effect of the cold coupled with relaxation of the protective muscle spasm, makes movement easier.

Ice Massage

As the name implies, ice massage is the movement of ice over the skin of the involved area. The ice is moved in a circular or back and forth pattern until the part is numb, approximately 5–7 minutes later. If the melted ice is wiped off the skin as it collects, numbness will occur sooner.

To obtain large pieces of ice that are easy to handle, fill styrofoam cups with water and freeze them. Leave the ice in the cup during the ice massage but peel down the edge. (See Figure 1.) The styrofoam serves as an insulator and protects the fingers from the extreme cold. Place a tongue depressor or spoon in each cup before freezing and use it as a handle during application.

Ice massage is not recommended for the immediate treatment of new injuries. Although cold penetrates deeper with this technique than with an ice pack, only a small area at a time can be treated. In addition, compression cannot be utilized in the control of swelling. Ice massage is usually used as a prelude to range-of-motion exercises.

Superficial Heat Modalities*

Superficial heat modalities are heating agents that penetrate no deeper than the skin and the underlying dermis at most. Although superficial heat modalities are

---

*A modality is any physical agent used therapeutically in the treatment of an injury.

a. Frozen cup.

b. Peeling edge down for application.

Figure 1. Ice cup for ice massage.

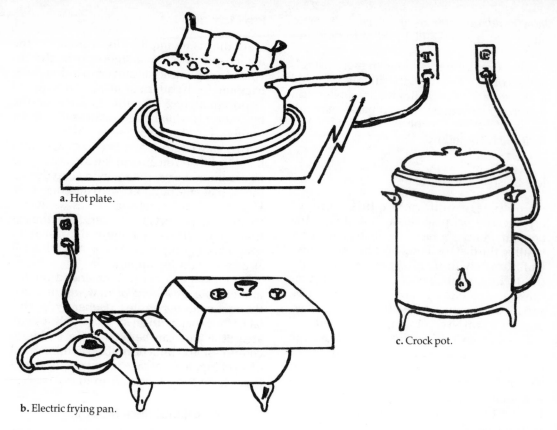

a. Hot plate.

c. Crock pot.

b. Electric frying pan.

Figure 2. Methods of warming a heat pack.

dangerous and should not be used without prescription by a physician, deep heat modalities such as ultrasound and diathermy are far more dangerous with regard to the tissue trauma either can create. Neither of these deep heat modalities should be used by anyone other than a trainer or physical therapist and not without a prescription.

Hydrocollator Pack (Heat Pack)

A hydrocollator pack is a canvas pouch filled with silica gel that absorbs heat. It is heated in hot water prior to use so a pack can easily be prepared at home on the stove, a hot plate, or other heating device. (See Figure 2.) Follow the manufacturer's directions for heating and storage of the used pack. Packs are available in various sizes for use on different body parts. Check at a local drug store or medical supply company.

Treatment time is approximately 20 minutes. Caution should be exercised when placing a pack on the affected area. A pad of at least six towels should be put between the pack and the exposed skin area. (See Figure

3.) In addition, because of the weight of the silica gel, the athlete may not be able to tolerate the weight of the pack on a recent tender injury.

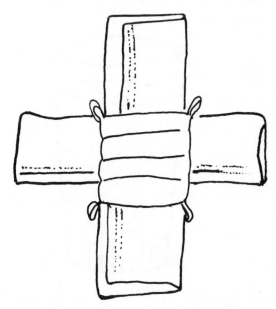

Figure 3. Using folded bath towels to insulate a heat pack.

Whirlpool

A whirlpool promotes relaxation by means of mechanical agitation of the water via the turbine. Relaxation is enhanced as the water temperature approaches 110° F. The water temperature should never be higher than 115° F as this poses a danger in burning the athlete. Cold temperature whirlpools have also been used in the treatment of new injuries to the extremities. Here the physiological effects of the cold as well as the buoyancy of the water, both of which are useful when the athlete attempts to regain range of motion, are used to the fullest potential. One advantage of the whirlpool is that the water temperature, hot or cold, changes very slowly, so the temperature remains constant through the length of the treatment.

Treatment time varies according to the part being treated. For an extremity, treatment time for a hot whirlpool ranges from 20–30 minutes. With half or full body immersion, treatment time should be no longer than 15 minutes. Treatment time for cold whirlpools is not as long—the colder the water temperature, the shorter the treatment time. When the part is numb, treatment should be terminated.

Never leave an athlete unattended in a hot whirlpool especially if one half or more of the body is immersed. The individual could faint and, if left alone, the results could be tragic. Always turn the turbine on and off for the athlete receiving the whirlpool treatment.

Whirlpool treatment produces a beneficial effect in the following conditions: musculoskeletal inflammation; both acute (cold whirlpool) and subacute (hot whirlpool); burns; open wounds; post cast immobilization; muscle spasm.

Combined Heat and Cold Treatment — the Contrast Bath

A contrast bath is used to gain the physiological benefits derived from both heat and cold applications. However, as with any heat modality, a contrast bath should not be used until swelling is controlled, 48–72 hours after the injury occurred. The local application of heat followed immediately by cold produces an active contraction and relaxation of the blood vessels which is helpful in removing stubborn swelling. The heat causes the blood vessels to dilate and the cold causes them to constrict creating a milking action that forces fluid out of the affected area.

There are several different time schedules used in this form of therapy. Regardless, two large containers and a clock for the set-up are needed. (See Figure 4). One container

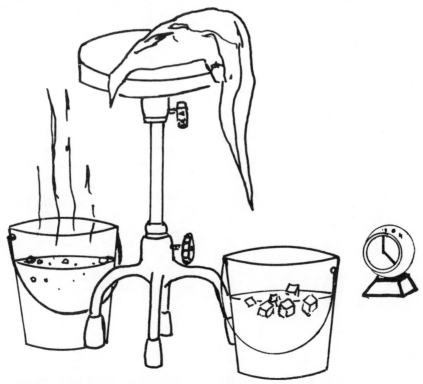

Figure 4. Set-up for a contrast bath.

should be filled approximately two-thirds full with hot water so that the temperature levels out between 105–110° F. The other container should be filled with cold water, the final temperature ranging from 60–70° F. The treatment is begun by immersing the part in hot water for ten minutes. From that point on cold and hot immersions are alternated four times. The affected part should be kept in cold water for one minute and in hot water for four minutes. The total treatment time is 30 minutes and should end with a hot water immersion. This schedule is ideal if followed by a massage treatment. Some of the swelling may then be manually forced out of the area. With another time schedule, the treatment starts and stops with cold immersion. By ending with cold immersion, the blood vessels are constricted and there is little change for additional swelling to occur. Total treatment time is 25 minutes with cold and hot immersions alternating every five minutes.

Contrast baths have been employed with success in the treatment of sprains and fractures (post-immobilization) of the ankle, foot, hand, and wrist. Strains have also been effectively treated with contrast baths.

Rehabilitation

Andi Seger, A.T.C.

4

To discuss the principles and concepts of rehabilitation, the term rehabilitation must be simply and basically defined. Rehabilitation in the case of sports injury is a total program of reconditioning, and in some cases, conditioning of the athlete following a traumatic or chronic injury. While this program is sometimes considered separately from a treatment program, the rehabilitation process begins immediately after the injury occurs, so this process is actually inclusive of the term "treatment program." There will be times though, that a rehabilitation program may have to be instituted at a later date as in the case of an injury occurring during vacation periods or an injury that should have been seen and treated, but was never given proper care. As a general rule, the longer an athlete is out of activity, the longer the rehabilitation process. Excessive immobility or rest of an injured body part may actually delay the healing process. The rate at which the athlete begins to regain mobility and begins to exercise the body part will in large part be based upon the physician's instructions.

Anyone responsible for supervising a rehabilitation program should keep in mind the primary objective of such a program, i.e., to get the athlete back into full activity as soon and as safely as possible. An accelerated rehabilitation program to get the athlete back into full activity before fully recovered can only result in further injury, possible permanent disability, or a different type of injury to either the same or another body part.

A second objective and equally important is to realize that an athlete who is out of activity for more than a few days will suffer a decrease in overall conditioning, and in particular, cardiovascular fitness. Within the limits of the physician's prescribed activity level for the athlete during the rehabilitation process, the program must be structured so that the athlete will be able to work on maintaining or increasing strength, flexibility, and cardiovascular endurance. If the program is not structured as above, the athlete may return to activity and competition at a lower level of fitness and be unable to perform at one hundred percent capacity. It may also result in another type of injury due to this decrease in conditioning level.

When planning and supervising a rehabilitation program, there are several areas that must be considered. The first of these is the psychological effect of an injury to the athlete. In dealing with an athlete's psychological state of mind, the most important fact is to be realistic with the athlete. The exact nature of the injury and the approximate length of time the athlete will be out of practice and competition (if known) must be understood by the athlete. He/she must also be made aware of the type of rehabilitation program that will be gone through and must understand why it is important that the program be followed exactly. The athlete also needs to realize program goals and that the success of the program will depend upon the quality and intensity of work at each step along the way. The harder the athlete works and the more dedicated he/she is, the better the results. So that the athlete achieves the goals set for him/her, the program supervisor can do several things. Specific work times should be established so that the athlete knows that he/she is expected at designated times. The supervising individual should also ensure that the athlete is following the program as he/she should and that the exercises are being correctly done and that progress is recorded. Finally, the individual supervising the program should be able to provide encouragement to the athlete, so that the athlete will continue to work hard. This individual does not have to be the coach or the staff trainer. A responsible student in the form of a student trainer or manager should be able to do this, if knowledgeable about the program and its purposes. It is sometimes difficult to keep an athlete motivated, especially if the program will last a considerable amount of time, whether it be several weeks or several months. If the athlete feels that he/she is still an integral part of the team, it becomes much easier to keep him/her highly motivated. In cases in which the athlete has an injury that will not keep him/her out for the entire season, it is advisable to have him/her attend at least part of every practice, even if unable to participate in most of the practice. As the athlete progresses through the program, he/she should begin to gradually work into practices, doing those activities which will not have a chance of furthering the injury or causing some other injury. The athlete must also be aware that when ready to return to competition, he/she may be behind in skill level depending upon the amount of time lost. An athlete that has been out several weeks may assume that he/she will immediately go back into a starting position. This will frequently not be the case, and the athlete should be made aware of this. With an injury lasting two weeks or less, the athlete will usually be able to immediately regain position as long as the fitness level has been maintained. After recovering from a moderate to severe injury, the athlete may be fearful about reinjuring the body part even though it is safe to fully participate. He/she may especially feel this way when repeating the same type of movement that caused the injury in the first place. This is a problem that must be taken care of by instilling confidence in the athlete and by sometimes pushing the athlete. In this case it is most important that the coach and/or trainer be aware of the emotional makeup of the athlete should this problem arise.

A second area that must be considered when organizing and supervising a rehabilitation program is determining why the athlete was hurt. If the athlete may have been hurt because of a suspected strength or flexibility deficiency, then the recurrence of a similar injury may be prevented. Several different questions arise when looking at the cause of an injury: Was it unavoidable, having nothing to do with the level of conditioning?; Was there a lack of general or specific flexibility?; Was it a recurrence of an old injury that was not completely rehabilitated?; Was there a strength imbalance between the agonist and antagonist muscle groups?; Was it the overall weakness of muscles and/or muscle groups? If it can be determined that one of the above problems existed and might be the cause of the injury, then the problem must be corrected so that future problems, or possibly more serious problems, are avoided.

A third area to consider is the sport itself. Different sports place varying levels of stress on muscles, tendons, ligaments, and joints, and the rehabilitation program must be planned accordingly; the program must be specific to the sport. For example, in a sport that requires a great deal of leg muscle endurance, the rehabilitation program must not only build sufficient strength and general endurance of the leg muscles, but should also put extra emphasis on leg endurance. In severe injuries, the athlete may also be forced to give up a certain sport in favor of another sport that might place less stress on the injured area. With this type of injury, the athlete should be made to understand that staying in the current sport may be questionable.

When designing the actual rehabilitation program, several different areas must be included: range of motion; strength; endurance; speed; agility. The regaining of motion and flexibility is the first area of concern. As a basic rule, the athlete should have full range of motion of the injured body part before rebuilding strength. The decision must be made as to when to start on range of motion, and in some cases, especially in moderate to severe injuries, the physician will make this decision. If the athlete has been in a sling, cast, or splint, motion will usually be begun as soon as the physician eliminates immobilization. A physician may also permit the athlete to remove a sling or splint several times a day to begin regaining of the range of motion. In less severe injuries, motion may be begun following the acute phase of the injury, which normally lasts from 24-72 hours post-injury. The end of the acute phase is marked by stabilization of pain and swelling and sometimes by a noticeable reduction of swelling. If motion is started and the body part becomes increasingly painful, or becomes increasingly swollen, then the regaining of motion must be curtailed until the part can be exercised without increasing the inflammation in the area. It may take an additional day or even several days before the athlete can again begin range-of-motion exercises. As soon as the injured area can tolerate the exercise, range-of-motion exercises can be performed daily.

There are different techniques of regaining range of motion, a few of which are somewhat complex and require background depth in exercise therapy. The easiest method, and most commonly used, is to have the athlete spend a couple of minutes every hour simply attempting to move the injured body part through the motions the body part normally goes through. The regaining of full range of motion may take anywhere from one day to several weeks depending upon the extent of injury and the length of any immobilization. The progress of the athlete should be checked daily, either through the use of a goniometer or by visual observation.

When full range of motion has been regained, the athlete must begin work on rebuilding muscular strength and endurance. There are many different types of equipment available on the market today that will accomplish this. A key concept to remember is that the program in which an athlete works, and the way in which the program is worked, is more important than the type of equipment used. Regardless of how sophisticated the equipment is, if it is not properly used and the athlete does not work to his/her potential, increases in strength will be negligible.

Several principles are involved when working on any type of strength program. As the athlete begins the program, he/she should be working daily strength-building sessions. Once the athlete reaches a plateau where he/she is no longer making steady strength gains, he/she should then switch to working three times per week. This plateau may be reached within several weeks or several months depending upon the injury. When the athlete has regained at least original muscular strength and endurance, a maintenance program may be used. If the athlete performs a good quality workout at least one day a week, the strength gains will be maintained. If lack of muscular strength is suspected as the cause of the injury, the athlete should continue working three times per week until appropriate strength has been obtained. Because of the lack of strength norms for women, this will usually involve guesswork on the part of the individual supervising the rehabilitation program. If the women athletes have been involved in a weight-training program for pre-season conditioning then that should at least provide a baseline to work from in deciding whether the injured athlete is below the average strength of the other women athletes. Whether it be the actual rehabilitation program or a maintenance program, the athlete should be working to maximum level as long as he/she is relatively pain-free. Muscular pain when working hard is common with all but a few types of exercise equipment, and this is to be expected. If more than minor pain occurs at the actual injury site during the workout, the athlete should work just below this level to prevent irritation of the injury.

There are three basic types of strength-building programs: isometric; isotonic; isokinetic. Regardless of the program, exercises should be based upon the type and location of the injury. If the injury is to a specific joint area, exercises should be given to strengthen all the muscles surrounding this area. The exercises should also be specific to the way in which the muscles are used in the athlete's sport.

An isometric strength program is based on building strength against resistance without a change in muscle length. It is frequently used as a strength-building technique when the injured body part is immobilized or is lacking complete range of motion. If used in this manner, it is usually recommended that the athlete do ten repetitions at six seconds each hour. The program may also be used to build strength after the athlete has regained full range of motion, but this is not employed as frequently. Most individuals involved in strength work agree that isometrics are specific to joint angles when building strength. Therefore, the exercise should be worked at three or four different angles throughout the entire range of motion with three to five repetitions of six seconds each at these angles. An isometric program has two advantages: it does not require equipment; the exercises can be worked in any direction. Two main disadvantages of the program are that improvements are not easily monitored and muscular endurance is not increased to any significant degree.

An isotonic strength-building program is based on moving the body part through the entire range of motion against some form of resistance. This resistance may be in the form of sandbags, dumbells, barbells, and weight machines. Although there are a variety of programs in terms of sets and repetitions, the most commonly used for rebuilding muscular strength is three to four sets of six to ten repetitions. For rebuilding muscular endurance, the weight is lessened and two to three sets of fifteen to twenty-five are most commonly used. The amount of weight used in either case can be found simply by trial and error. The athlete should be able to barely complete the last few repetitions of each exercise. Once the prescribed number of sets and repetitions has been reached, the weight is increased. Full range of motion must be stressed on each repetition and each repetition should be done slowly and correctly, taking four to six seconds to complete. Isotonic exercise can be easily recorded and improvement is readily seen. It also has the advantage of eccentric lengthening as the weight is slowly lowered. This is termed negative work and research has begun to show that negative work may be just as effective or even more effective in building strength as positive work or concentric contractions. The primary disadvantage is that isotonic exercise does not work the muscle at maximum potential throughout the full range of motion. It does not adjust to the differing levels of strength potential found at different angles throughout the range of motion.

The program of isokinetics involves fixed speed of movement throughout the full range of motion. With an ioskinetic device the speed of movement is set and the athlete exerts as much force as possible against the lever arm. Three sets of ten repetitions are used for building strength and two to three sets of twenty are done for endurance. Since many of the isokinetic units come with read-out dials, endurance work may also be done until less than 50% of the first reading is reached. A primary advantage of ioskinetic exercise is that the athlete can exercise at the speed of contraction necessary for specific sports skills. In addition, it is not uncommon for an injury to be the result of a deficiency of muscular strength in only one segment of the range of motion. Other advantages are that improvement is easily recorded and work on an isokinetic unit creates very little muscular soreness. The main disadvantage is the absence of the ability to perform negative work on this type of device.

Once range of motion, strength, and endurance have been returned to their original levels, agility will return as the athlete works into practices. Specific drills that are normally included in practice sessions will enable the athlete to regain the necessary agility level.

Cardiovascular fitness, the last area to consider, is extremely important. While it is best if the injured athlete can begin working on this immediately, the type of injury may dictate some possible contraindications. For example, even with an upper body injury, running and/or jogging may be contraindicated, especially during the earlier stages of the rehabilitation program because of the amount of jarring associated with it. Bicycling and swimming are two alternative programs of cardiovascular fitness that may be used. Some type of cardiovascular program should be started as soon as there is no chance of creating irritation or inflammation of the injured body part.

In deciding when and if an athlete is ready for full practice and competition, several guidelines are used. In the case of a moderate or severe injury that has been seen by a physician, the physician should make the decision. With an injury not seen by a physician, the coach or trainer will usually make the decision. Even with an excellent rehabilitation program, there is always the question of whether the injured body part will withstand the rigors of full competition. With a severe injury this is sometimes a question that even the physician will not have to answer. The athlete may be cleared to participate but may find that the body part cannot withstand the stress placed upon it. To avoid this problem, the coach or trainer should isolate the sports skills and have the athlete demonstrate that he/she can perform them at his/her pre-injury level before being permitted to participate in practices as well as competition. As the athlete progresses through the rehabilitation program there will be a gradual increase in his/her ability to perform the necessary skills involved in his/her specific sport.

Along with the athlete being able to perform the skills involved in the game there should be an objective analysis of the athlete's range of motion, strength, and endurance. The basic criteria for return to competition is achievement of 90-100% strength and full range of motion. In the case of an extremity, strength and range of motion should be measured by comparing the injured with the uninjured body part. Endurance of the body part should also be tested by bilateral comparison, with the criteria being equality of strength at 20-25 repetitions. The endurance test is vitally important because the athlete's maximum strength may be equal; if the muscular endurance is not equal, the body part, particularly when dealing with the knee, may be reinjured.

If the above criteria have been met and the athlete is in good cardiovascular shape, he/she should be able to safely return to competition. It must be remembered that at this point, the athlete should be put on a program to ensure the maintenance of the acquired muscular strength and endurance.

Athletic Conditioning 5

Kathy Heck, A.T.C.

A well-conditioned athlete has several advantages over a less-fit competitor. Athletic fitness ensures greater resistance to injury, improved skill execution, and an increased tolerance for work. Programs designed to build and to maintain athletic fitness consist of three major components:

- flexibility—range of motion of the joints;
- strength—the ability of muscles to exert force against resistance;
- endurance—the ability to persist.

In developing such programs the competitive year is divided into four seasons:

- pre-season—the four to eight weeks prior to the beginning of a competitive season;
- in-season—the competitive season itself;
- post-season—a 10-14-day "R & R" or rest period following the end of the competitive season;
- off-season—the period of time between post-season and the beginning of the pre-season period.

Conditioning activities vary according to the time of the competitive year. If the athlete engages in several sports throughout the year, there is overlap among the conditioning seasons. However, the basic principles still apply.

In the off-season period athletes should be instructed to build a conditioning base. This includes long, slow distance running of 30 minutes or more, stretching, and weight-training three to five times weekly. The off-season is also the time for basic skill work or for major sport technique changes to be made. While the athlete is away from the pressures of the competitive season, such changes can all be accomplished much more effectively.

With a good strength and endurance base developed in the off-season, the pre-season conditioning period emphasizes work specific to the athlete's particular sport and/or position. Endurance work is directed at the type of staying power needed in the sport itself, e.g., base-running drills for softball, fast break drills for basketball, speedwork for sprinters in track, etc. Weight-training is continued to build and to maintain strength, and flexibility work is also increased.

In-season training is directed toward the maintenance of athletic conditioning, strategy, and sports skills. To build fitness, workouts must be conducted a minimum of four to five times weekly. To maintain fitness, two to three workouts per week are required. The post-season break is not always possible for multi-sport athletes. But it does provide a much-needed vacation from the conditioning routine.

Flexibility

The body is a series of levers (the bones) moved by the shortening and the lengthening of the muscles. If the muscles are not as elastic or as flexible as they should be, efficiency and skill execution is hindered. Sedentary living and the increases in body fat that tend to accompany that lifestyle, serve to decrease flexibility. Flexibility is best developed and maintained through daily static stretching exercises. The calves, quadriceps, hamstrings, low back, groin, trunk, shoulders, and neck are the areas of particular importance. It is important to stretch prior to exercise to give the body an adequate warm-up. This is vital to the prevention of muscle strains and ligament sprains. Muscle soreness following activity can also be greatly reduced by stretching after an exercise session. Flexibility training should be done on a daily and year-round basis.

The technique used in static or slow-tension stretching is to stretch the appropriate body part to the point of tightness, hold that position for 15-30 seconds, relax, and repeat 3-4 times. Bouncing (ballistic) stretching is a dangerous technique and should never be used. Receptors in the muscles are stimulated by fast, jerky movements, and the resulting effect is contraction rather than relaxation and lengthening of the muscle tissue. Bouncing may result in over-stretching, soreness, and injury.

Flexibility Tests

Can the athlete:

- touch the palms to the floor while keeping the legs straight?;
- complete a shoulder grip exercise in both directions?;
- touch the nose to the knee while doing a hurdle stretch?;
- touch the knee to the floor while doing a quadriceps hurdle stretch?;
- complete a wall push-up with the body at a 45° angle and the heels on the floor?;
- touch the knees to the floor while doing a groin sit?

If so, the athlete is relatively flexible and needs only to maintain his/her present level of flexibility. If not, stretching should be done 2-3 times daily. A good source of flexibility routines is the book *Stretching* by Bob Anderson.

Endurance

Endurance is the ability to persist, and it is dependent upon one's cardiovascular (C-V) fitness. A simple gauge to determine improvement in one's cardiovascular fitness is a decrease in the resting heart rate. As C-V fitness improves, the heart rate decreases and the amount of blood pumped with each beat (stroke volume) increases. Therefore, the heart is beating less often, but each contraction is more powerful and more efficient. A change in the resting heart rate should appear 6-8 weeks after beginning a regular exercise program. The average heart rate is 72 beats per minute, but this is a highly individual matter. Many athletes involved in endurance-type sports have resting heart rates in the low 50s or high 40s.

The resting heart rate can be determined by taking one's pulse at either the radial artery in the wrist or the carotid artery in the throat. The body must be at rest for approximately five minutes prior to taking the resting rate. Count the heartbeats for 15 seconds and multiply by four. The heart rate can also be used to monitor the intensity of an exercise session by using the following formula:

$$
\begin{array}{ll}
220 & \text{(base number)} \\
-20 & \text{(age)} \\
\hline
200 & \\
\times.80 & \text{(80\% of maximum capacity)} \\
\hline
160 & \text{(maximum exercise heart rate)}
\end{array}
$$

Subtract the subject's age (for example, 20 years of age) from the base number of 220. Then, multiply that number by 80%, since a young, healthy individual should be exercising at approximately 80% of his or her maximum capacity. The resulting number is the maximum heart rate that should be achieved during an exercise session. To build or maintain C-V endurance one must exercise:

- strenuously enough to elevate the heart rate to 120-160 beats per minute;
- for a minimum of 20 minutes;
- at least 3-5 times weekly.

The pulse rate must exceed 120 beats per minute for the exercise to be of any C-V benefit, but it should not exceed the maximum exercise heart rate of 160 beats per minute. The individual should exercise to the point of fatigue, check the pulse rate, and as soon as it drops to 120 beats per minute, resume exercise. Scientifically, one's C-V fitness is based upon the maximum amount of oxygen that can be utilized by the body. The techniques used to determine maximum oxygen consumption, VO_2, are costly and time-consuming. Therefore, Dr. Kenneth Cooper, M.D., the author of *Aerobics**, developed the 12-minute run test to estimate maximum VO_2 capacities of athletes. Quite simply the athlete runs as far as he or she can on a track for 12 minutes. Dr. Cooper's book offers charts to determine fitness levels according to 12-minute run tests results. This test is most beneficial when used as a pre-, in-, and post-season gauge of the athlete's fitness. It is accurate and easy to administer.

Running for conditioning should preferably be done on grass or on a soft track. Soft surfaces reduce the jarring effect that running has upon the body. Good shoes are vital. They must fit properly and have good arch support, a firm counter, and a wedge heel. Use good running form: knee action

---

*Cooper's latest book in the Aerobics series is *The Aerobics Way*.

high; arm swing relaxed; body erect; head up; eyes forward; rocking up on the toes from the heel. Never run down hills; run up and walk down. Keep in mind that swimming and cycling may be substituted for running. According to Fox and Mathews in their book *Interval Training* the activities can be compared in the following manner:

Activity	Time	Distance
Running	8:00 minutes	1 mile
Swimming	8:00 minutes	¼ mile
Cycling	8:00 minutes	2.5 miles

Long, slow distance work should be done in the off-season. As competition nears, times and distances should be altered to make the endurance training more specific to the individual's sport.

Strength

Strength can be built or developed in a variety of ways. The most common techniques are calisthenics, where the body's own weight is used as a form of resistance such as in push-ups or sit-ups, and isotonics, where weights are lifted. Weight-lifting is the fastest and most efficient means of developing muscular strength. Some general principles of weight-training include:

- lifting should be done on alternate days;
- the lifting activities should build strength needed for the athlete's sport(s);
- good form is necessary—the individual should train, not strain;
- a proper and complete warm-up is necessary;
- provide specific sets, repetitions, and workload progressions for the athlete;
- chart progress via record-keeping;
- safety must be emphasized at all times.

Many techniques are used to determine the loads and repetitions for weight-training. The most common is the DeLorme technique. The athlete determines the maximum weight he or she can lift 10 times. Then, the individual completes three sets of 10 repetitions at 50%, 75%, and 100% of the 10-count maximum weight. In all cases the overload principle must be observed; without placing an overload on the body it will not respond with increasing strength. The DeLorme technique ensures that the amount of overload will be within the individual's ability range and will train, not strain, the muscles.

Strength training is crucial in the prevention and the rehabilitation of athletic injuries. It is important and safe for both male and female athletes and can lead to safe, improved performances by all.

The basic principles of conditioning are summarized in the following timetable.

Conditioned athletes have an inherent advantage over their less-fit competitors. Improved, safer performances are desired by all athletes. Athletic conditioning is hard work, but its benefits are many.

	Strength	Flexibility	Endurance
Off-season	3× weekly Build	Daily Maintain	3-5× weekly Build Base
Pre-season	3× weekly Build	2× daily Build	3-4× weekly Specific to sport
In-season	2× weekly Maintain	Daily Maintain	2-3× weekly Maintain

Protective Equipment and Devices*

Holly Wilson, A.T.C., Ph.D.

Protective equipment is necessary to control those hazards of the sport that cannot otherwise be eliminated. All too often injuries occur because standard protective equipment is of poor quality, improperly fitted, or in disrepair. To avoid many problems, purchase equipment only from an authorized dealer. Before a decision is made, discuss specific needs with representatives from various manufacturers. The coach, athletic director, team physician, and trainer should evaluate each piece of equipment before the order is made. In general, the size, strength, and skill level of each athlete should be considered when ordering and assigning equipment.

Before each season, review with the athletes the importance of protective equipment. Emphasize why it must be worn as well as properly fitted and in good repair. Show the group how to properly use and care for each piece and how to make a quick inspection for defects. Check with the manufacturer or sales representative for recommendations concerning cleaning and maintenance of equipment. Many detergents break down plastic, so conscientious cleaning with the wrong substance may actually reduce the protective quality of the equipment.

During the meeting is also a good time to review the team rules, a few of which should concern equipment, e.g.:

1. Protective equipment must be worn at all times during practices and games.
2. Protective equipment must not be modified without the prior consent of the coach, trainer, or team physician.
3. Protective equipment must be properly used and not abused.
4. Any defects in personal equipment must be immediately reported before activity is started.

Since protective equipment varies from sport to sport, it is not possible to include guidelines here for the fitting and care of each piece. When available, follow the manufacturer's recommendations for fitting and care. There are however, a few pieces of equipment used in almost all sports that are rarely considered equipment, much less protective equipment. Both athletic shoes and eyeglasses should be thought of as protective equipment. A mouthguard, which is frequently used in many sports, is also discussed here.

Athletic Shoes

Although the choice of shoes is usually the decision of the athlete, that choice should be based on sound reasoning rather than due to the whim of the athlete. The coach should provide the athlete with some important pointers about selecting athletic shoes. During activity the stresses placed on the feet, which in most cases are still growing, demand more than the minimal support provided by less expensive shoes. Injuries may be minimized by the correct shoes. In football, susceptibility to ankle and knee injuries is markedly decreased when soccer shoes are worn instead of the conventional football cleats. In basketball, high-top shoes provide additional support for the unstable ankle. Shoes for racket sports and basketball should be reinforced along the forefoot. This reinforcement not only prolongs the life of the shoe but also provides more support and protection for the foot. In running shoes, particularly those designed for training, sta-

*The copyright for this article has been retained by the author. Similar material will appear in the book, *Coaches' Guide to Athletic Training*, which has been accepted for publication by Human Kinetics Publishers.

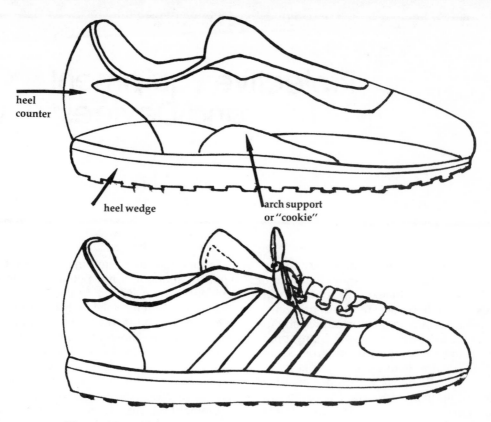

heel counter

heel wedge

arch support or "cookie"

Figure 1. Running Flat

bility and support are sacrificed as more cushion is added to the midsole. Items to consider when choosing any shoe for athletics include the support and snugness offered by the heel counter which should be firm, the fit and firmness of the arch support, and the thickness and flexibility of the sole, especially the forefoot. (See Figure 1.) If the shoes are going to be used on a hard surface, the soles should be somewhat flexible. On an irregular surface, the soles should be stiffer, perhaps with a steel shank. Waffle or ripple sole shoes are designed for straight forward movement, not lateral changes of direction, since the likelihood of an ankle sprain increases with such movement. The heels should be level, not tilted inward or outward, when the shoes are placed flat on the table.

Fitting Athletic Shoes

Regardless of the type of shoes worn, they should fit properly and provide good support for the feet. Shoes should be fit in the afternoon when the feet are swollen to ensure accurate sizing. In addition, the same number and type of socks worn during prac-

tices and games should be worn when trying on the shoes. Shoes should be fit to the length of the arch rather than the length of the athlete's foot. Fit can be checked easily and quickly. The ball of the big toe should be directly over the widest part of the shoe when the athlete is standing. (See Figure 2.) If it falls in front, the shoe is too short. An abnormal crease in the shoe along the inner arch confirms this finding. The break of the shoe, where it bends on push-off, should be at the widest part of the shoe. Check both feet for one may be substantially larger than the other. Fit the shoes to the longer foot. If the shoe is not comfortable, it does not fit. In reality, the shoe will break the athlete in; the evidence is blisters, corns, and calluses.

Care of Athletic Shoes

It is more than likely that the shoes may become saturated with water sometime during the season. If so, fill each with crumbled newspaper and allow the leather, canvas, or nylon to dry out slowly. Slow drying delays deterioration of the shoe. If warranted, apply a coat of saddle soap to the shoes when thoroughly dry.

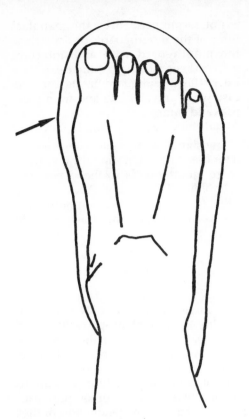

Figure 2. Correct shoe fit.

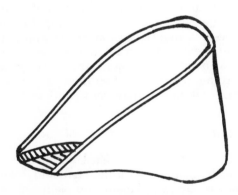

a. Padded.

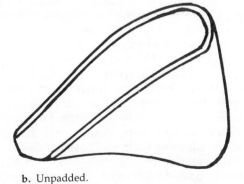

b. Unpadded.

Figure 3. Commercially-available heel cups.

Shoes should never be washed in the washing machine or dried in a dryer. Either one causes premature deterioration of materials—fabric as well as bonding between layers.

Heel Protection

Some running shoes have a plastic heel cup incorporated into the shoe as the counter to absorb and spread the repetitive pounding on the heel when running. Unfortunately, a bruised heel may occur in sport activities other than running and attempts to protect the tender area are often for naught unless a heel cup is used. A vinyl foam doughnut cut to conform with the shape of the heel rarely provides adequate protection. Plastic heel cups, padded or unpadded, may be purchased at many sporting goods stores. (See Figure 3.) If the protection afforded by the unpadded heel cup, or even the padded heel cup, is inadequate use $1/4$-$3/8''$ vinyl foam to line the inside surface, and cut back on activity!

Corrective Lenses

Athletes who need prescription lenses to correct an eyesight problem should not rely on street-worn frames and lenses for eye protection in sports. Wire-rim frames and glass lenses are particularly dangerous. Such frames and lenses are not designed to withstand the stress and may actually cause an injury to the eye. Prescription lenses should be ground of industrial plastic and set in either an industrial or sports frame, or, some type of goggle with a Lexan-injected molded lens may be worn over prescription glasses. Contact lenses, either hard or soft, do not provide any protection for the eye. Soft lenses are recommended over the hard type, however, only because they stay in place better. If an athlete must wear contact lenses for proper vision, the individual should wear some kind of protective eyewear. Most of the eye protectors worn in racket sports that do not have lenses interfere with peripheral vision. Such protective devices are adequate only in badminton and tennis where the size of the missile is too large to enter the orbit of the eye. Only in badminton may street-worn glasses provide adequate protection against damage from an aerial missile.

Mouthguards

Although mouthguards are not as common to sports as athletic shoes or eyeglasses, they are common to most contact/collision sports and play an important role in preventing lacerations of the mouth, fractures of the jaw/teeth, and concussions. The mouthguard imparts the force of a blow to all teeth rather than localizing it at the point of impact. Consequently, the mouthguard should always be worn whether the athlete is just participating in a drill, scrimmaging, or competing in a game. Many athletes dislike mouthguards (and refuse to wear one) because they feel that mouthguards are uncomfortable and interfere with breathing as well as with speech. In most cases, these problems are minimal and are far outweighed by the protection the mouthguard provides. If the mouthguard is particularly troublesome, check the fit. It may have been improperly fitted.

Two types of mouthguards are generally used in athletics. The mouth-formed is commercially available in junior and senior sizes while the custom-fit is molded by a dentist or an oral surgeon. The mouth-fitted mouthguard is momentarily heated in boiling water and then the athlete molds the semi-pliable plastic form to the bite. Caution the athlete not to bite too hard for the teeth could go through the plastic form. When properly fitted, this mouthguard is tight enough to stay in place by itself. Breathing and speaking may be affected but only minimally. Custom-fit mouthguards are more comfortable and interfere less with breathing and speech than the commercial ones but are more expensive. Consult a local dentist or an oral surgeon for details concerning cost. Since an impression of the bite is made, the mouthguard fits exactly and stays in place. A custom-fit mouthguard is recommended for an athlete with braces, a bridge, a plate, missing teeth, or an odd-shaped dentition.

Regardless of the type of mouthguard worn, it should be trimmed only to alleviate abnormal rubbing. The tips should be no shorter than the last molar. Too much trimming reduces the effectiveness of the mouthguard as a protective device. More important, the trimmed mouthguard may become a hazard for it could be swallowed and obstruct the airway.

Care of Mouthguards

Like any other piece of equipment, a mouthguard should be well-cared for so that it lasts several years:

- Store the mouthguard in a liquid solution. Consult a local dentist if a solution

is not recommended by the manufacturer of the mouthguard, or daily rinse the mouthguard with a disinfectant wash to keep it odor-free and clean.
- Keep the mouthguard in its carrying case when travelling to and from practices and games.
- Avoid chewing on the mouthguard.

At the first sign of wear, mold a new mouthguard for the athlete. On trips always carry a few spare mouthguards so that a new one can be molded if necessary. Above all, enforce the team rule that the mouthguard must be worn whenever the athlete is on the playing field.

Improvising

Protective equipment can adequately serve its intended purpose only when it is good quality equipment, properly fitted, and in good repair. Even when these requirements are met injuries do occur which, in some instances, necessitate a modification in standard equipment. Such modifications may require only the addition of more padding for protection of the tender area or they could be more complex requiring the improvisation of a protective pad.

Sometimes protective equipment is not commercially-available in the proper size so a facsimile must be custom-made. This practice is especially true as more girls and women are competing in athletic programs. Existing equipment often does not fit their smaller stature or anatomical configuration.

Materials for Construction of Pads

Different materials are used for padding a sensitive area—adhesive felt and foam, foam rubber, vinyl foam, and plain felt. The choice of material is dependent on the severity of the injury, its location, and the tenderness of the area to be padded. Because foam spreads the force as well as absorbs it, it can be advantageously used to protect areas subjected to repeated impact such as the heel or ball of the foot. However, the various types of foam have different force-absorption capacities. Vinyl foam provides the most protection in comparison to adhesive foam and foam rubber. It is the material of choice when padding bruises (contusions). The air cells in adhesive foam and foam rubber collapse under force permitting the two surfaces to come into contact. Thus the force of the blow is transmitted directly to the underlying tissue requiring protection. Vinyl foam, on the other hand, has such absorption capacity that the two sides rarely come near one another. Unfortunately vinyl foam is expensive and it is not available except in large sheets. Smaller pieces of vinyl foam might be available at a local medical supply company, orthopedic brace shop, or from a local orthopedic surgeon or podiatrist. The most useful sizes of padding material for injury protection or prevention are ½'', ⅜'', ¼'', and ⅛'' thicknesses.

To reuse a vinyl foam or foam rubber pad, trim the tape from around the edges of the pad. If the athlete attempts to pull the tape off, the pad usually rips. Continue to reuse the pad until it has lost its cushioning effect due to the tape build-up. Use the old pad as a pattern to make a new one.

Sheets of plastic air bubbles, commonly used as packing material can be used to pad some flat areas such as the thigh or forearm. Unlike vinyl foam or foam rubber, the sheets of bubbles cannot be reused. At the end of an activity period a majority of the air cells have collapsed which reduces the pad's protective quality. Large rolls of the packing material are available from various manufacturers but it may be possible to acquire a smaller quantity from a local store that regularly ships fragile merchandise.

Felt, like foam, spreads the force, but it does not absorb it. It does, however, provide support, so felt is used in the construction of arch pads. It is also used for doughnut or horseshoe pads to protect blisters, corns, or plantar warts because the natural sliding action of the foot in the shoe tears up a foam pad. Another advantage of felt is that it can be split into different thicknesses. Divide a corner of the felt sheet at the desired thickness and carefully but firmly pull the two layers apart. Felt pads, especially those made from wool felt, are quite durable and can be reused for several days. (Trim the tape from around the edges as for a foam pad.) Wool felt withstands ''packing'' from weight-bearing pressure better than cotton felt, but it is difficult to find in small quantities. Orthopedic surgeons and podiatrists frequently use felt in treating musculoskeletal injuries and may be willing to split an order or donate any scraps. Prepackaged assortments of felt may be purchased at many sporting goods stores that handle athletic training supplies. The felt squares come in a variety of thicknesses ranging from ⅛-⅜''.

Small squares of moleskin, adhesive foam, and adhesive felt (wool blend) are available at most local drug stores. Adhesive felt is available in a variety of thicknesses. Precut pads, including doughnuts, are also commercially-available in latex rubber or felt at most drug stores. Although the pads have an adhesive backing, adhesive tape can also be used to secure the pad in place. Unfortunately, precut pads are more expensive than homemade renderings and such pads can only be used once. In fact, it may be necessary to replace the pad before activity as well as after. Finally, a slight modification may be necessary in the precut pad before it can be used. Do not use medicated pads for any type of skin lesion unless instructed to do so by a physician. Not only do such pads tend to overmedicate but if improperly used, even healthy tissue can be damaged.

Construction of Pads

Frequently a pad must be constructed because commercial pads do not meet specific needs. In the long run, this practice may be more economical. When constructing protective pads, the following tips may be helpful:

1. The depth of the involved tissue determines the thickness of the padding material, e.g., if the area is swollen or covered with a thick callus, a thicker pad is needed. To estimate the proper thickness, apply gentle pressure with the finger to either side of the involved soft tissue.
2. Moisten the area to be padded with water. Outline it in indelible pencil and then press the padding against the area. The pattern transfers to the padding and serves as a guide for cutting.
3. Taper the edges of the pad to prevent them from rolling up or the pad from shifting as a result of shearing forces.
4. Proper placement of the pad is of utmost importance. If improperly placed, the resulting discomfort is often greater than that associated with the original condition. To ensure proper positioning apply manual pressure to the pad before taping it securely in place. The athlete should not experience any discomfort.

Certain materials have traditionally been used to construct the different types of pads. Moleskin cut in an oval shape is used to reduce friction between the ball of the foot and the shoe which decreases the chance of a blister developing. Such a pad is especially useful when the area is callused. (A small piece of gauze may be placed between the pad and the skin.) Adhesive felt or foam is used for the construction of doughnut pads;

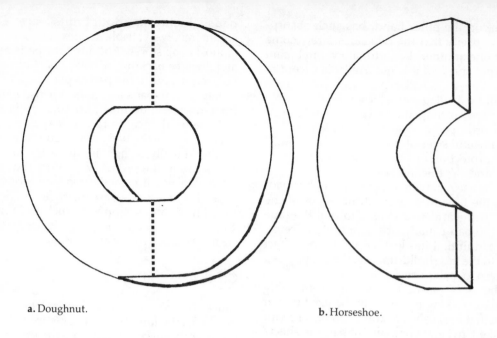

a. Doughnut.   **b.** Horseshoe.

Figure 4. Converting a doughnut pad to a horseshoe.

however, the doughnut has given way to the horseshoe in the protection of common foot ailments such as blisters, plantar warts, and corns. (See Figure 4.) With the natural tendency of the foot to slide forward in the shoe, the front edge of the doughnut "catches" thus increasing the stress at that point. When the pad is converted into a horseshoe, the back and sides of the lesion are still protected, but there is no front edge to "catch." Also there is no doughnut hole, a common site of discomfort as tender tissue is displaced downward into the hole. Commercially-made doughnut pads can be easily modified prior to application. Simply cut out a small wedge and then bevel the ends of the horseshoe. Bevelling allows the foot to freely slide forward with minimal restriction so that irritation is reduced.

Pads for bruises (contusions) are cut in the shape of a doughnut out of thick vinyl foam if available. (If not, fold a sheet of air bubbles into several thicknesses, put it over the tender area and secure it in place.) Several layers of material may be glued together to achieve the desired thickness; however, a special glue for use on rubber material must be used. The size of the cut-out piece should correspond to the size of the tender area. This is true when cutting any doughnut or horseshoe and some speciality pads.

For sensitive bruises (contusions) that are prone to repeated blows, a more durable pad is required. Hard-press board thigh pads, which were predominantly used in football prior to the introduction of vinyl-dipped pads, may sometimes be modified to provide adequate protection. Pad the underside with a doughnut, approximately ⅜'' thick, and glue the two together. Put the pad in place and cover it with an elastic bandage. Start the bandage just below the bottom of the pad and angle it up one side of the part and down the opposite side. Continue this "herringbone" pattern until the pad is covered. If available, secure the bandage with elastic tape. Start the tape at the bottom of the pad, applying it in a circular fashion around the affected part. Overlap each layer by one-half the width of the tape and make sure the entire bandage is covered. If necessary, to prevent the pad from slipping, apply a turn or two of tape around the part directly on the skin. If elastic tape is not available, apply a few strips of athletic tape around the part, two just below the top of the elastic bandage and two just above the bottom. These strips should not be too tight as the underlying muscles must have room to relax and contract or they may cramp.

Legal Liability* 7

Richard T. Ball, Attorney-at-Law

I. Litigation: Will It Destroy Athletics?

One of the most valuable environments in American society for the growth and development of young people is found in competitive athletics. There are opportunities in sports for valuable learning experiences which are not elsewhere available during the formative years and which provide excellent preparation for the rigors of life. Most important to those of us who engage in the teaching and coaching of school-age youngsters is the potential development of intangible characteristics such as working with others, accepting authority, developing self-discipline, and learning the important relationship between determination, hard work, and success.

A great and probably unfillable void would be felt should the competitive environment be destroyed. Indeed, any diminution of athletic programs reduces the number of youngsters who will reap rewards which might not otherwise be available to them.

Athletics Threatened with Destruction

The most common obstacle to solving a problem is denial that it exists. When a large segment of a society chooses to ignore or deny the existence of a threatening menace, the size of the obstacle increases, not in a linear fashion, but geometrically. By the time enough people awaken to the need for action, the damage can be irreparable and the result fatal.

For several years, a small but vocal number of concerned people have cried a warning to American society: "This precious environment, so important to our young, is being threatened with total destruction. Litigation arising out of athletic injuries is accelerating out of control and, if the tide is not turned quickly, the institution will crumble and fall."

For the most part, their warnings have fallen upon deaf ears. Society at large simply has not comprehended the relationship between "a few lawsuits" and the total demise of athletics. More frightening, most of those who live and work in and have deep love for that institution have chosen to deny that any such problem exists or that tragedy could result.

The time for awakening to reality has passed. Those who regard competitive athletics to be important must begin to take action immediately. In the belief that much of the tendency toward denial results from a lack of awareness of facts, this article will be designed to convey to the reader in-depth information concerning the nature of the problem, the reasons it exists, and what can be done to solve it. In the process of doing so, special attention will be given to exploring certain myths which have intensified the problem.

It is important to know how and why athletic injuries occur, what can and cannot be done to prevent them, what roles equipment and coaching do and do not play in their cause and prevention, and how all those related in any way to the American athletic environment can join together in a common cause to guarantee the continued healthy existence of competitive athletics.

An important aspect of this educational exercise is to correctly identify the problem and then work to keep that problem clearly in focus throughout the discussion. The difficulty encountered by most people is successfully separating facts from myths.

---

*Reprinted with permission of Cramer Products, Inc. and the author.

Rate of Severe Injury

The problem is not the occurrence of catastrophic injury or death in football or any other athletic endeavor. Despite the physical violence of the game, the rate of severe injury in football is extremely low. Statistical studies show that within the same age group a young athlete is exposed to far less risk than in common environments, particularly vehicular transportation and even in the home. Naturally, severe injury rates in other sports are even lower than football. While it is possible that careful attention to conditioning programs and teaching techniques may reduce the injury and death levels even further, no degree of care or concentration will absolutely eliminate severe injury from the athletic scene.

The problem is not with athletic equipment and, more specifically, the football helmet. The gravest crisis to the future of athletics resulting from litigation has arisen within the football helmet industry. All football helmets currently on the market are doing an excellent job of performing their assigned task. The National Athletic Injury/Illness Reporting Survey reveals that over a 3-year-period there is not significant difference in the levels of severe head injury among the various helmets on the market today. It is a fact that head and neck injury in football are not related to the equipment being worn by the injured person. The same is true of similarly serious injuries in wrestling, gymnastics, baseball, and other sports where serious injuries and deaths have occurred.

Economic Impact of Severe Injury

The problem which must be dealt with is the economic impact caused by litigation which is founded in emotion and poor judgment rather than rationality and fact. Protracted litigation brought by young athletes who have suffered debilitating injury in athletics and which involves years of preparation, the testimony of numerous medical, scientific, statistical, and athletic experts from all over the country, and requires several weeks of trial, is creating a burden which manufacturers and schools will soon be incapable of bearing—particularly in this age of intense concern about tax reform and the repeated tendency to cut back athletic programs first when attention is given to economizing in education. Unless a rapid change is made, the cost of maintaining athletic programs will become too severe and the institution will indeed disappear.

Many people are prone to attack the judicial system and its traditional procedures as the culprit. Such an approach is misguided. It is important to America that a forum exists in which an aggrieved party may present a case for recovery against one responsible for the loss and be justly and fairly recompensed. The problem arises from misuse of that process. It is magnified by those who come forward in the court of law and render professional opinions concerning the cause and mechanism of injury and the manner in which that cause might be eliminated without having developed adequate support for those theories.

The potential in football and other sports for violent impact of human bodies against one another or against fixed objects is great. Any high energy impact can result in severe injury. Many times severe injury creates an extreme economic need.

Repeatedly, in litigation involving athletics, physicians, engineers, and even coaches have come forward with theories concerning injury cause and mechanism for which they have no support. Any testing performed has been minimal and the interpretation placed upon the results of those tests questionable. However, they are too often accepted as fact.

Jurors are laypeople, often uneducated in medical or scientific matters and frequently without the ability to truly understand the testimony of these experts. Because of the tremendous emotion generated by the sight of a young athlete who has been rendered a quadriplegic or suffered the destruction of mind and body through injury to the brain, the plaintiffs and their attorneys are able to make a strong argument that the opinions of these well-meaning experts who fault the athletic equipment for the tragedy should be accepted and a substantial reward given to the injured person.

The existence of injuries and lawsuits does not establish that athletic equipment is poorly designed or manufactured. To the knowledge of this writer, claims against manufacturers universally involve a charge that the equipment was improperly designed. They do not arise from instances where the equipment failed as a result of some manufacturing defect. It must be understood that there are limitations to the degree of protection to be enjoyed from a piece of athletic equipment. A gymnastics mat is not and cannot be designed to absolutely protect a gymnast who dismounts from a high position and lands incorrectly. Football helmets are not and cannot be designed to protect the neck, and they are even incapable of preventing most of the severe injuries which can occur to the brain in the football environment.

Cost of Lawsuits

Many people find it difficult to understand how litigation against schools and helmet manufacturers can possibly threaten athletics. Very few cases have been tried and even the number which have been filed and which have been settled, or are still pending, is extremely low when compared with suits for example, against the automobile industry.

Bear in mind that the protection sought against the potential for lawsuits arising out of injury which the injured claim others caused is the purchase of insurance. Insurance carriers charge premiums which are based upon their prediction of the financial risk to which they are exposed. Even though there are probably only 50-60 lawsuits currently pending against all helmet manufacturers, many of these involve neck fracture and quadriplegia from severe injury to the brain. One verdict alone in Dade County, Florida, was in the amount of $5.3 million. Another more recently rendered in Philadelphia was in the amount of $600,000. While writing a policy of insurance and charging a premium, the carrier must have in mind those potential losses.

More significantly, even the cost of winning these lawsuits is enormous. The cases of catastrophic injury which have been tried against football helmet manufacturers reveal that the expense of preparing a case and taking it to trial will usually exceed $100,000 and may very well be 2-3 times greater. When multiplied times the 50-60 lawsuits which are pending and an undetermined number which might be brought in the future, it can be seen that the insurance industry faces a tremendous potential expense from this relatively low rate of suit experience.

As a consequence of these expense risks, the premiums charged to the manufacturers of athletic equipment have escalated to astronomical levels within recent years. Some are now paying premiums 50-100 times greater than they were four years ago. There are football helmet manufacturers who currently pay in excess of $1 million, and for some this involves coverage requiring a substantial out-of-pocket expense on each claim by the manufacturer itself before the insurance coverage even becomes effective. Where the risk of loss appears to the insurance company to be too great, coverage is simply refused, and the manufacturer must then bear the cost of defense and payment of claims out of its normal operating budget.

Whether the cost involved is for insurance premiums or self-insurance, the effect is a tremendous increase in the cost of doing business. The only available means for dealing with this problem is to increase the price of the product. This effect is transmitted immediately to the schools. Obviously, there is no way that schools will be able to bear unlimited increases in the cost of football helmets, baseball batting helmets, wrestling mats, gymnastics mats, and other equipment.

Schools and Litigation

The schools themselves are far from being free of problems created by litigation. In many suits involving catastrophic injury in the athletic environment, the coach and the school are named as defendants. This again brings into play the problem of insurance coverage and its cost. The school is then caught in the position of having to pay both for the manufacturer's insurance coverage (through the increased price of equipment), and the cost of its own insurance. Obviously, the public is not going to tolerate unlimited budgets for this purpose.

The solution to the problem is education of those who are directly or potentially involved in the litigation process. The tide of litigation will not be stopped by force. The general public can do nothing to prohibit insurance companies from charging higher premiums. If that risk becomes too great and the company decides not to write the insurance, this again is beyond the control of the public.

Certainly, manufacturers cannot be prohibited from charging prices for their products which are necessary to cover the cost of doing business as it is increased by the risk of litigation. It is doubtful that the federal government will be willing to underwrite the cost of either the claims or the manufacturing of athletic equipment.

There is a limit to the ability of our economy to tolerate the rising costs and consequently the answer must be in stemming the tide of the lawsuits themselves. Only when people within the athletic environment, including parents of athletes, medical people who treat athletic injuries, engineers who design athletic equipment, and the public at large understand the full scope of this problem and become willing to do something about it, will a solution be found.

In the following paragraphs, attention will be directed to the particular facets of the problem and the efforts which can be made by coaches and other school personnel to effect a solution.

Checklist for Coaches

A brief checklist is provided below for coaches to employ during their sport season. This may eliminate some potential problems.

1. Meet with parents and athletes as a group before practice begins or as early in the season as possible, and explain all the risks involved in the game. Stress that everything possible has been done to reduce those risks. Advise that equipment cannot totally eliminate them. Despite all efforts and the efforts of all coaches across the country, a few participants will be seriously injured every year.
2. Stress the values of the game which justify the risks and the far greater risks which are present in other common activities.
3. Make sure the parents understand the program, and keep the door open for questions and comments.
4. Make sure the equipment is safe, sound, and in good condition. All helmets should meet NOCSAE specifications.
5. Distribute to each player a written copy of the rules related to the use of the head in blocking or tackling. Stress these rules daily, especially in tackling situations.
6. Be alert for and, if necessary, eliminate from the program, players who are not adequately prepared physically, mentally, and emotionally for the violence of the game.
7. Give special attention to the development of neck strength, particularly in players using heavy helmets.
8. Make every effort to have present at every practice a person properly qualified to deal with severe injury who has no other responsibility. This would preferably be a certified athletic trainer. In any event, know how to discern and properly deal with severe or potentially severe injury, especially to the head and neck at all practice sessions.
9. Have a physician qualified in sports medicine present at every game.
10. If severe injury occurs, don't panic. Remind parents, press, and all concerned that no one is to blame. Make no speculative statements about how the injury occurred. Store any equipment involved and any films or photographs of the incident. Notify the manufacturer of the equipment involved immediately. Have the school seek the counsel and advice of a lawyer knowledgeable in the athletic injury field.

II. Catastrophic Injury: Why Must It Be?

Rising costs imposed by the need to defend suits in which athletes seek huge sums of money for injuries will eventually force schools out of athletics if change is not effected. Attention was called to the urgency for discouraging use of the judicial system as a response to fatal or totally disabling injury.

No athletic injury gives rise to such dramatic public concern as injury to the brain and spinal cord. An understanding of the mechanisms by which these trauma occur will not only aid in reducing the risk of those which are avoidable, but enhance understanding and acceptance of the fact that some annual incidence is inevitable.

Not Isolated to Football

The risk of head and neck injury is not specific to football. In baseball, death or disability from brain trauma, usually inflicted by thrown balls, is a yearly occurrence, and severe neck injury, usually from collisions on the basepaths, is a realistic threat. The potential for severe head and neck injury is present in wrestling, gymnastics, swimming, and diving—any sport involving rapid body movement.

A notion prevails that the greatest risk of injury to the brain comes from impact of its surface with the bony interior of the skull. Ayub Ommaya, M.D., acting chief of neurosurgery at the National Institute of Health, has spent several years attempting to dispel this misconception.

While he does not minimize the importance of trauma to the surface of the brain, Dr. Ommaya points out that most of the injuries produced in this fashion have little, if any, long-range effect. Of grave concern are those injuries which result from rapid rotational movement of the brain, particularly when combined with movement of the skull in a different direction or at a different rate.

Causes of Concussion

The original Latin term from which the word concussion was derived was literally translated as "shaking about of the brain." Because it is a sizable mass, precariously perched atop the much smaller spinal cord, under certain circumstances the brain possesses the characteristics of a ball on a whip. The fact that it literally floats in cerebrospinal fluid, a liquid with properties and behavior much like water, enhances this response. Such an effect only occurs if the mass is rapidly set in motion.

Obviously, a blow to the head may initiate this process. A sudden blow to the body may also cause rapid acceleration of the head with resultant "whipping" of the brain. This physical experience is most often observed in rear-end automobile accidents, with their infamous whiplash injuries. This injury is no less possible in sports, particularly football, where there may be violent and often unexpected blows to the body which suddenly set the head in motion or change the direction of its motion. The helmet is in no way involved.

Concussion may vary in severity from brief, transient loss of neurologic function (being "stunned" or having one's "bell rung") to more serious incidents of prolonged unconsciousness and amnesia. What has not been understood, and what Dr. Ommaya's research has verified, is that these variances are determined by the depth in the brain at which the shaking phenomenon (concussion) is experienced. If the physical movement is mild, the effect will be felt only on the surface, and the neurologic consequence will be slight. As the violence of the shaking increases, the effects are experienced more deeply, posing the greatest risk. The tearing of sensitive tissues in the brain with resultant bleeding and development of permanent scar tissue leaves the victim in a lifelong compromised condition.

The important thing to understand is that no blow to the head, much less impact to the skull, is needed to cause concussion. O.J. Simpson once commented that he had experienced two concussions during his football career, both of which occurred when he jumped to catch a pass, had his legs undercut, and landed solidly on his buttocks. We all relate to the experience in boxing of a highly effective knockout punch being delivered to the point of the chin. These are just two examples of concussion which occur when the head is suddenly and violently jerked. No blow to the skull is required.

Subdural Hematoma

The vast majority of the brain injuries which have plagued football and stimulated lawsuits are not concussions. The most common occurrence is the *subdural hematoma*. In this injury the initial severe trauma is not to the brain at all, but to blood vessels which lead out of the brain. It is, however, initiated by the same type of sudden rotational acceleration which leads to concussion.

The veins in the brain pass out of the top and sides of the brain through the *dura,* a fibrous sheath which is loosely attached to the skull, and which houses the cerebrospinal fluid.

Although the space between the surface of the brain and the dura is not large, under sudden, violent movement, the brain stiffens and literally bounces within the skull cavity. If this occurs, the veins are stretched and a shearing stress is applied.

Under virtually all human experiences, the veins tolerate this stress without serious result. On rare occasion, however, the shear stress will be too great and the veins tear. The result is bleeding into the space which is designed to contain only cerebro-spinal fluid. Because this gathering of blood (hematoma) is in the area below (sub) the dura, it is denoted as *subdural hematoma.*

The brain is capable of accommodating a slow, mild development of such blood, often without any observable side effects and usually without severe problems. This is known as a *chronic subdural hematoma.* If, however, the bleeding is more profound the effects will be felt within 48 hours. This is a potentially fatal occurrence and is called an *acute subdural hematoma.*

Because of the similarity in body movement which sets the two injuries in motion, there will virtually always be some degree of concussion when the veins are torn. Consequently, the player is compromised to some degree immediately. Very often, however, this is a very mild concussion, which is followed by a lucid interval, during which the player may perform without readily discernible problems for a period of minutes or perhaps hours. Once the intracranial pressure caused by the bleeding becomes too intense, the player will begin to evidence serious neurologic symptoms and very quickly become comatose. This is a life-threatening circumstance and usually must be surgically treated within 30-60 minutes if the patient is to survive.

The subdural hematoma is not to be confused, either in description or mechanism, with the *epidural hematoma* which also appears annually in fatality and injury statistics, primarily involving baseball players. The latter injury, which develops more rapidly and is fatal a greater percentage of the time, involves a gathering of blood *above* the dura in the very minute potential space between that fiber and the skull. In this instance, the damaged vessels are arteries, which bleed more rapidly than veins. Because there is no opportunity for rotational movement, such trauma results only from inbending or fracture of the skull.

If there were truth to the allegations of a few physicians and engineers that football and baseball helmets are woefully inadequate, allowing direct blows to the skulls of players, there would indeed be an epidemic of epidural hematomas. On the contrary, the rate of such injuries is extremely minute. As previously indicated, statistical studies reflect that all helmets on the market are doing an excellent job of preventing all brain injuries, and especially these deadly epidural traumas which are really the only severe risk which a helmet can eliminate.

Fracture/Dislocation of the Neck

One of the saddest misconceptions ever developed advocates a relationship between football helmets, gymnastics mats, or other padded protection, and fracture/dislocation of the neck with resulting quadriplegia. Dr. Ommaya reports that he is unaware of a single instance of neck fracture from a blow to the head where the victim's head and body are stationary at the moment of the blow. It seems that movement of the body is essential to fracture/dislocation of the neck. Albert Burstein, Ph.D., director of the Biomechanics Department at the New York Hospital for Special Surgery, gives a most logical explanation for this observation.

Dr. Burstein explains that when bones break or joints are disrupted, the force causing the injury can be a direct blow. More often, kinetic energy developed within the body will cause the force. This is virtually always true of neck injury.

Kinetic energy (measured in foot pounds) is defined in engineering as the ability to do work, and is created when a body (mass) is set in motion (velocity). The greater the weight of the body and the faster it moves,

the more kinetic energy it possesses. When this energy comes to a stop, the result is the creation of force.

According to Dr. Burstein, these biomechanical principles explain the neck fractures and dislocations in athletics. A foot pound of kinetic energy is described as one pound of body weight dropped from a height of one foot. Obviously, a 150-pound gymnast dismounting from a high bar six feet off the ground develops a tremendous amount of energy before hitting the mat below (900 foot pounds!). Similarly, a 150-pound football player running at top speed develops a great deal of energy, especially if diving to make a tackle. In either case, tremendous force is developed when the body stops.

Because it is a jointed skeletal structure, the entire human body does not stop immediately upon impact. For example, when a gymnast dismounts incorrectly and lands head first, the head will stop, but the body will keep moving. We are speaking of time factors in milliseconds, but if the neck is the point where the force will be applied when the energy of the trunk of the body comes to a stop, the gymnast is in grave trouble. The direct application of only 8-10 foot pounds of energy will fracture the neck. Here the energy transmitted may be hundreds of foot pounds.

Design of the Body to Absorb Energy

Fortunately, the body as a whole, and the neck in particular, does an excellent job of absorbing energy and reducing the force transmitted to the bones and ligaments. The joints of the skeletal system are designed to bend substantially in one direction in order to bring these soft structures into play. Consequently, if the gymnast can quickly tuck so as to land shoulder first in a rolling fashion, the neck will not be severely injured. If the football player's head is erect and as it stops the neck is hyperextended—the direction in which the joints in the neck are designed to bend—the muscles and other soft tissue will absorb the energy and the bones and joints will not be damaged.

It is only when the neck is positioned so that the vertebrae are in a straight column and the joints cannot bend in response to the transmission of energy that severe damage occurs. This happens if the head is nodded forward only slightly and is grossly exaggerated if the chin is brought down onto the chest. In a flexed position, the joints of the neck will buckle under excessive load. The damage may be to the bones and/or ligaments. If the result is too much movement of the vertebrae, the spinal cord is traumatized and paralysis occurs.

The important fact to understand about this process is that the risk to the neck is the force created by energy of the body. According to Dr. Ommaya, energy contained in some outside mass which impacts the top of the head would have to cause damage to the brain and skull before breaking the neck. Such damage is not present in the case of neck fracture/dislocation and quadriplegia suffered in athletics. Dr. Burstein points out that if the energy which causes the injury passed from the head into the neck, the damage to vertebrae would be in the first and second vertebrae rather than at the lower levels which have been involved.

Furthermore, logic dictates that the amounts of energy contained in the body under circumstances such as those involved in football, wrestling, gymnastics, and swimming and diving is the cause of neck fracture.

Understanding these mechanisms of brain and neck injury makes obvious the impossibility of absolutely eliminating them.

Susceptibility

Obviously, anyone who puts his or her body into a position where massive amounts of energy are transmitted directly into a straight, stiff neck or suffers a horrendous uppercut blow which sets the head into a rapid rotating movement, may well suffer a tragic result. Some people, because of a unique physical weakness, will be more susceptible to injury.

The intent here is to educate, not encourage a negative, fatalistic attitude. Attention must always be given to the great benefits of the athletic experience. Life is not, and never will be without its risks. There is not more justification for concentrating unnecessary attention on this negative aspect of the athletic experience than on any other phase of living.

There is, however, reason to bear in mind that involvement of the head in contact is the common denominator in both types of catastrophic injuries. By constantly reminding and teaching players not to use any part of the face or head as a primary point of contact, football coaches will take great strides toward eliminating the preventable injuries from the game.

This is not to say that players should not keep their heads erect and move into a block or tackle with their eyes always on the target. As pointed out above, the neck is best able to handle stress if it is extended and upon impact bends to the back. However, it is imperative that the primary application of force not be to the face or neck. At the instant contact is made, the head must be slipped to the side so that force is applied to the shoulder.

It is also imperative that the neck musculature of players be as well prepared as possible to bear the stress imposed. A strong, well-developed neck will not prevent neck fracture if too much force is applied to the bones, but will aid the player in keeping the head properly positioned at all times.

Symptoms

Equally important is for the coach to be alert to those situations where the catastrophic injury may have occurred. Usually the neck fracture/dislocation causes immediate paralysis, but this is not always true. The player may suffer an injury to a joint which causes pain, but no apparent disability. If properly handled, the athlete will recover without serious problems. If, however, he/she is sent back into contact, the result could be tragic.

The player with a subdural hematoma would demonstrate minimal evidence of injury at first. However, these minimal signs act as a warning to be on the alert for more severe problems and to take every precaution for the player's well-being. Any player who has experienced a violent, sudden movement of the head followed by any concussion symptoms must be watched very carefully for 24-48 hours and should be examined by a neurosurgeon. This observation may include waking the athlete several times during the night to check responses. Diagnostic tools are now available by which the presence of a developing subdural hematoma may be discovered before the problem becomes critical.

The need for the presence of a certified athletic trainer at all practice sessions and for a physician qualified in sports medicine at all games is poignantly accentuated. It is hoped that with the foregoing general explanation of the biomechanical factors involved in such injuries the coach will be better able to avoid those occurrences which increase the risk of such tragedies and to deal with them if they occur.

III. Capabilities and Limitations of Protective Equipment

Design Considerations

The designer of equipment must consider such factors as the economic position of the buyer, usefulness, comfort, durability, and the users' acceptability of the product. A designer must also carefully consider *trade-offs*. Every product has certain advantages and disadvantages. By designing to eliminate one danger, the manufacturer may create another; by selecting material suitable for one purpose, the manufacturer may create a problem by using the product for other purposes.

Baseball helmet manufacturers have struggled with these problems for years. Initially there was great resistance to wearing such a device at all. Even today, players refuse to wear a helmet which they don't consider light, comfortable, attractive, and convenient. In light of these problems, it is difficult to design a helmet which adequately protects against a ball which may be pitched at speeds above 100 mph.

A different kind of dilemma is confronted by the manufacturers of mats for wrestling and gymnastics. The manufacturer is required to strike the delicate balance between a mat which protects against injuries and yet allows freedom of movement. If the mat is too thick and soft, movement will be hindered.

Manufacturers of eyeguards for handball, racquetball, and squash have faced litigation in which it was claimed that injury occurred to the eye despite the wearing of the eyeguard. The only way to guarantee that no contact will be made with the eyes is to totally cover them. The use of glass would pose risks, and there is no plastic available which does not seriously impair vision. Narrow eye openings are safer, yet they impair vision. By over-designing, the manufacturer may eliminate use of the protection altogether.

Football as a Dilemma

Football manufacturers are confronted with the most complex dilemma of all in considering the factors and trade-offs involved in equipment design. The same type of headgear will be worn by people ranging from high school freshmen to adult professionals, will be kept on players' heads for 2-3 hours per day, 5-6 days per week, over a period of 3-4 months, and will be used in blistering heat and freezing cold, humid and dry air, rain and snow, in mud and dust, on grass, hard-packed dirt, and carpet-covered concrete. Helmets used daily in practice must also present an attractive appearance on game day. The equipment must be strong enough to resist the impacts, yet light enough to be safely worn, give coverage to as much of the head as possible, and not restrict the vision, hearing, or movement of the player.

Over the years, manufacturers have learned that the trade-offs involved in varying helmet styles can be extreme. The strap suspension system is an excellent protection concept because it aids the head in effectively moving away from a blow to the helmet. However, to function effectively, the suspension is required to fit tightly and can't be modified to accommodate unusual skull shapes. In an effort to solve these problems of comfort and fit, padded systems were developed. These helmets were hotter, heavier, and did not move the head away from the blow. The protection given was excellent, as long as there was still compressibility in the padding; once it became entirely compressed, the padding was as hard as the shell. In an effort to accommodate this problem, helmets with a combination of air, water, and padding were developed. These provide both fit and protection, but are out of necessity, extremely heavy and frequently in need of the repair or replacement of parts.

The most interesting irony about the varieties of helmets which have been developed and the trade-off factors involved is that statistically it has been proven that the protection given by all helmets on the market today is the same . . . regardless of the protective system. Since all helmets give the same high level of protection, a coach or athletic director must decide which is the most practical and functional and what trade-offs are involved.

If players wear an exceptionally heavy helmet, they must develop the neck muscles to avoid fatigue which might result in the player putting his/her head into positions which create a risk to the brain or neck. If a team is to use a helmet with padding which completely encircles the head and has no space for the flow of air, players must remove the helmets frequently so that the head can cool and the body heat can be reduced. It can readily be seen that there is no simple answer to the problem of design or selection of the "best" football helmet.

Helmet Failure

While there is occasionally a clear and obvious failure of a particular product, those situations usually involve comparatively minor injuries. There is not a single lawsuit known to the author alleging massive brain injury or neck and spinal cord injury in which the helmet involved is said to have failed. The serious cases all involve claims that the *design* of the product is inadequate to give the required protection, or that the design contributes to the injury. It is the contention of the plaintiffs in these cases that every unit of that particular model of equipment has exactly the same defect. The attacks which have been made on protective athletic equipment have virtually always come from people who are outside of both manufacturing and athletics.

It is also important to bear in mind that these attacks upon athletic equipment are always theoretical; they are based upon laboratory experiment, rather than the actual experience in the athletic environment. Most often the person attacking a football helmet does so by way of comparing it to a different helmet, which in laboratory experiment produces results which are allegedly better.

Essential to the opinions of these so-called experts is a great deal of speculation regarding the levels of tolerance of human beings to injury. It is not known precisely at what level of force concussion or other damage occurs to the brain, nor can it be determined precisely how much energy was involved in a blow which caused a particular injury. To say that a certain amount of increased protection would have prevented the injury requires pure speculation.

Claims against Manufacturers

The oldest and broadest claim against manufacturers in cases of catastrophic injury relates to the energy absorption capabilities of the equipment involved. As pointed out in the second section of this series, once the body is in motion, it possesses kinetic energy which must be expended. As the energy comes to a stop, it creates force, the magnitude of which is governed by the time and distance over which the body stops moving. The attackers say that protective equipment can and should be designed to effectively reduce the force and thus eliminate injuries.

Manufacturers have attempted to discover the ideal material for use in helmets to bring the energy of a blow to a stop before it reaches the skull and brain. One self-appointed expert has proposed that the ideal padding for all helmets is a material consisting of polystyrene beads. This is best described as an extremely dense styrofoam and is used in vehicular crash helmets. It was used in the Cougar and Bell Toptex football helmets, and proved so unacceptable that they are no longer on the market. In fact, in one study the rate of low-level concussion with this type of helmet was dramatically increased.

The author believes that head injury is head injury, and head protection is head protection, inasmuch as the brain does not know the source or nature of the energy input which might cause it injury. Consequently, all helmets should be tested in essentially the same fashion. The test circumstance advocated by this individual is derived from a standard for vehicular crash helmets.

This would mean that all helmets would be virtually identical, regardless of the purpose for which they're used. The presence of a firm crushable liner is virtually essential to meeting this standard and it is almost impossible to design a functional, practical helmet for football which would pass such a test, much less for baseball, hockey, skiing, bicycling, and other such activities.

A second concept advocates the employment of a soft outer shell for all football helmets. This is primarily advanced as a means for protecting other players from blows administered by the helmet, but some theorize that increased protection will be enjoyed by the wearer. Those who advocate such a modification have engaged in no testing to determine the effects to the neck and brain of the wearer of the helmet from such a change in the surface of the shell.

The most damaging attack upon protective equipment, particularly football helmets, gymnastic mats, and wrestling mats, relates to catastrophic injury of the neck resulting in spinal cord damage and paralysis. Here again, the analysis has been made that the equipment contains inadequate energy absorption capabilities and if properly modified the injury could be avoided. Because it is always impossible to determine the amount of energy and resultant force which was involved in the injuring impact, such experts are forced to compare the equipment involved with some alternative equipment, compare the energy absorption performance of the two pieces of equipment, and then speculate that with the increased energy absorption the injury would not have occurred.

Another self-appointed expert has propounded the theory that the posterior rim of most football helmets can impose a force upon the neck in a manner similar to a guillotine and thus cause dislocation/fracture of the neck. The claim here is not that the mask is used as a handle to jerk the head of the player around, but rather that because it protrudes too far, a mechanical disadvantage is created upon the neck as a result of the additional leverage. The author alleges that when the helmeted head is rapidly extended to the rear, the posterior rim of the helmet strikes the neck with excessive force. Once again, this opinion was obtained and expressed without a shred of concrete medical or scientific evidence existing in its support.

Equipment Manufacturers' Responses

The industry's response to these attacks has been diverse. In all instances, manufacturers remind both the attackers and the athletic public that they must look at the full spectrum of considerations. Of extreme importance is the design and marketing of a helmet which players can and will use, and which will serve all of the purposes for which it is intended. Design engineers in the helmet industry carefully evaluate the trade-offs, determining every problem which might be created in an effort to solve some other problem. Finally, it is essential that all people concerned recognize the limitations upon the ability of equipment to protect against injury and the inadequacy of our knowledge about the actual tolerance levels of athletes to injuries.

As explained in the second section, concussion and subdural hematoma injury are caused by rapid rotational acceleration of the brain. So long as the head is free to move suddenly backward and forward, these rotational phenomena can occur. Only by stabilizing the head on the shoulders could such a risk be eliminated. Obviously, a helmet of that type would be totally non-functional for the game of football. To attempt eliminating rotational movement with padding would require a helmet 6-8 inches thick.

With respect to football helmets, it is important to bear in mind the potential ultimate capabilities of the equipment to give protection. The only purpose a helmet can serve is protection of the scalp and skull. Skull fractures and the epidural hematomas which would occur with inbending of the skull are non-existent in football. Many experts claim that the plastic of the shell deflects under certain high energy loads in football, causing the shell to come in violent contact with the skull. If this were true, skull fractures and epidural hematomas would be epidemic in number.

The suggestion that energy absorption material would help prevent neck and spinal cord injuries demonstrates a total lack of understanding of the biomechanics involved. As previously explained, fracture of the neck is caused by force transmitted when the energy of the body comes to a stop. The problem which exists is that the athlete is moving in a head first fashion and suddenly the head slows down or stops while the body keeps moving for a few milliseconds. The force generated when the body comes to a rest is then imposed upon the neck, which cannot tolerate that force. To solve this problem with padding would require that the head be slowed or stopped more gradually and in concert with the body.

How much distance would have to be involved for this to be accomplished? It is known that in cases of neck fracture suffered by trampolinists, they came down on top of their head in the middle of the trampoline. The webbing of the trampoline deflects as much as two feet before it is stretched to its maximum capacity and stops moving. At that point, the head comes to a rest but the body is still moving with sufficient energy to break the neck. If two feet of stopping distance is insufficient, how can one conceive of developing a padding for a football helmet or gymnastic and wrestling mats which would solve the problem? The answer is obvious. *Football helmets are not, never were, and never will be designed to protect the neck from fracture.*

The suggestion that the configuration of the helmet shell and/or facemask causes fracture of the neck likewise demonstrates ignorance of biomechanical principles as well as medical facts. In the first place, there is no reported case in which the claim is made that the victim's neck was broken by the rear rim of the helmet acting as a guillotine *and* in which that victim had any bruising on the neck. Since far less force is required to bruise the skin than to fracture the bones of the cervical spine, this defies logic.

Secondly, it is impossible to bring the posterior rim of the helmet into contact with the cervical spine without releasing the chin strap and moving the helmet out of its normal position on the head of the wearer. Anyone involved in football realizes that when the chin strap is released, the helmet comes off.

Finally, radiographic motion picture evidence has recently been produced involving hyperextension movements by volunteers wearing football helmets, which positively establishes that when the head is extended backward, the rear rim of the helmet proceeds down and away from the cervical spine and does not move in toward the cervical spine. If it eventually comes in contact with the back of the wearer, it does so at a point no higher than the seventh cervical vertebra. All of the cases of neck fracture/dislocation in football involve injury between the third and sixth cervical vertebra.

The suggestion was made to the football helmet industry that to avoid this risk, the posterior rim of the helmet be cut one inch higher. The one manufacturer who complied with this design suggestion is involved in a multi-million dollar law suit brought by a young man who suffered quadraplegia in a football game wearing that helmet; the allegation is that the rear rim of that helmet caused the neck fracture. Also, elevating the back rim exposes the extremely vulnerable occipital area to blows which can be fatal. No available foam padding can adequately protect against such blows.

Facemask Involvement in Injury

Testing recently completed by design engineers reveals that the size and shape of the facemask have no bearing upon the amount of force experienced by the neck when the facemask is impacted. In all likelihood this is because when the facemask is lifted or pushed backward, the effect upon the head is always experienced only at the forehead and the chin strap. Until the chin strap begins to pull on the chin, the head does not respond to an upward movement of the facemask.

In all instances then, the force applied to the neck will come from the chin. The suggested change of moving the facemask closer to the face and making it releasable or collapsible would totally negate the protective capabilities of the mask. Players would be better off if the mask were completely removed so they did not receive a false sense of protection. *It would be questionable wisdom to take such drastic action in response to a purely speculative theory that the facemask plays a role in catastrophic neck injury.*

A soft outer shell, which would reduce injuries to those struck by a helmet, would mean extreme risk to the wearer. Testing within the helmet industry reveals that the forces to the brain and neck are dramatically *increased* when a soft covering is placed over the hard plastic shell. One of the great protective features of helmets is that most blows rapidly glance off the surface. This would no longer be true with a soft shell. Even if the surface were made extremely slick by the addition of some chemical coating, the dishing effect which would occur in the soft surface upon impact would still increase the amount of time of the blow; this has a direct bearing upon the force transmitted to both the brain and the neck. *A far more effective means for protecting players from the helmets of other players is to eliminate the use of the helmet as a weapon.*

While a perfect, totally protective helmet has not and cannot be devised, all reasonably conducted surveys of the protective performance of helmets on the football field reveal an excellent result. By increased awareness of the trade-off factors involved in various helmets, coaches can be certain of enjoying the maximum possible advantage from the head gear of their players.

It is also imperative that coaches, players, their parents, and the general public realize the inherent limitations upon the helmet to give protection, the fact that players and coaches can do as much as anyone to eliminate head and neck injury by avoiding the use of the head as a primary point of contact, and that unless there is a failure of the helmet shell with resulting damage to the scalp and skull, the helmet is not to be faulted in cases of injury to the neck and brain.

IV. Factors in Protecting Athletes: Equipment, Training, Medical Care

There are several steps to protection of the athlete, including equipment management, conditioning and training athletes, and appropriate medical care.

Examination of Existing Equipment

Old, worn-out, inadequate protective equipment must be replaced immediately. Unless a decision has been made to replace the entire inventory of equipment, the first step in selection involves careful examination of the equipment by a person of appropriate skill, background, and experience. This is usually someone involved in equipment manufacturing, sale, or reconditioning. Until the school has a full-time, carefully trained person whose sole concern is equipment management, there is no more reliable critic available than a representative of the sporting goods industry.

The recommendations of such a person must be carefully considered. Nothing is more alarming to a trial lawyer than to learn of recommendations for the replacement of poor equipment being ignored for economic reasons.

Selection of new equipment must also involve the advice of a trusted representative of the sporting goods industry. Any purchase should be negotiated only with an authorized dealer or representative of the manufacturer. The savings enjoyed in the purchase of equipment from "bootleggers" is heavily outweighed by problems which arise in exercising warranty rights, and obtaining parts for repair and maintenance or assistance in solving problems with the equipment. Acquisition of equipment through a "bootlegger" for economic reasons is also a fact which can and will be played upon by a plaintiff's lawyer in litigation which involves the school.

It is a mistake to select equipment without consideration of the size, strength, intelligence, maturity, and capability of the athlete who will use it. It is similarly incorrect to employ a protective device for one purpose when the intended purpose of the manufacturer was entirely different. For example, football helmets employing a suspension system which combines foam padding, water cells, and inflatable air chambers, were originally designed to accommodate problems of fit. A misconception developed among coaches, trainers, and athletes is that this helmet was developed to solve problems of concussion and was particularly suitable for a player who had suffered a head injury. These helmets are no better able to prevent concussion than any other, and to acquire them for that purpose is a mistake.

There is a marked difference in the weight of various helmets, and to safely employ the heavier models an athlete must have adequate neck strength. Many helmets by their design completely encompass the head with padding, allowing no room for movement of air. Heat elimination can only take place through evaporation and air movement. Any helmet which inhibits these processes must be employed with extreme caution in a hot, humid climate.

Of equal importance in the management of protective equipment is the process of maintenance, repair, and replacement on a regular basis. From the very start of the season it is critical to have an adequate supply of replacement parts. It is important that repairs take place immediately.

Because of constant use, equipment must be carefully inspected on a weekly basis. This again shows the need for a full-time person whose sole responsibility is the management of equipment. While athletes must be taught to make their own inspections on a daily basis, follow-up by someone more skilled and experienced is essential. There must also be an annual inspection, preferably at the close of the season, by a skilled consultant who can designate the equipment which needs reconditioning or replacement.

Very often athletes will take protective equipment home and make some modification which they think will improve its appearance or comfort. The result can be disastrous. If athletes understand the danger to which they expose themselves in using a device which is broken or worn-out, they will lend better assistance to the inspection.

Individual Suitability to Athletics

In training and conditioning athletes, attention must be given to the whole person, taking into consideration mental and emotional factors as well as physical characteristics. Not every individual is suited for competitive athletics. The best preventive measure with respect to some injuries is a "weeding out" process very early in the season. An opportunity to compete should be afforded every youngster willing to meet the conditions of participation. However, participation may indeed be harmful to some.

For example, a youngster with outstanding physical skill may have attributes of aggression or self-destruction which make his/her participation in contact sports an unreasonable risk. Other athletes possess such extreme fear of injury or failure that their judgment is impaired, thus increasing the risk of injury. Coaches must evaluate each athlete from the standpoint of the potential for individual growth from participation in sports.

Stressing emotional control and an intellectual, rational approach to athletics is as vital to prevention of injury as any aspect of physical development. All too often the catastrophically injured athlete is an unusually aggressive youngster who failed or refused to heed repeated warnings concerning the risks involved in certain activities or techniques. The philosophy of trying to hurt an opponent will often result in severe injury to the attacker rather than the intended victim.

Heat and Humidity

It is imperative that coaches be continually aware of the effects of the environment. Heat and humidity pose grave risks. Every football season is marred by the tragedy of deaths from heat stroke. The number of other injuries which are the result of excessive body heat is probably ridiculously high.

The U.S. Armed Forces have discovered that excessive body heat results in a loss of both physical coordination and rational judgment. The combination of the two leads to carelessness and clumsiness, the result of which can be a rash of various injuries to the head and orthopedic structure. This problem can be magnified by certain types of equipment, particularly helmets, unless appropriate precautions are taken.

The basic common solution to excessive body heat is an adequate moisture level in the body and cooling of the body surface. Any rapid loss in body weight (even two or three pounds) is normally a result of loss of body fluids. In hot, humid weather, the body needs all of that fluid to properly cool itself. Under such circumstances, practice sessions without frequent water breaks are extremely dangerous, and athletes must be not only allowed, but encouraged to remove their helmets frequently so that the head can cool.

Cold, Playing Surfaces, Fatigue, and Coaching

Cold weather likewise poses risks. The warmup process is of greater concern under such circumstances. In many regions the climate may dramatically change during the course of the season, and a coach must make appropriate adjustment in both practice and game situations.

Playing surfaces are known to pose varying risks to certain types of injury. For example, there is an indication that friction between the sole of the athlete's shoe and the surface of synthetic turfs is a major cause of injury to the knee. Dr. James Arnold, the team orthopedist for the University of Arkansas, reports that an epidemic problem of knee injury was solved in the Arkansas football program by simply wetting down the playing surface prior to practice.

Fatigue is another factor which can lead to serious harm. This again will be a cause of poor judgment and loss of coordination, but too often the athlete will not recognize his/her own limitations, or the fact that he/she has exceeded those boundaries.

Finally, special attention must be given to player techniques as a means of preventing injury. Particularly in football, the techniques used by players are responsible for catastrophic injury to a far greater degree than any other controllable factor. Use of the head as a primary point of contact in either blocking or tackling is an invitation to disaster. Players must be constantly reminded of

this fact and, if necessary, eliminated from the team rather than allowed to continue use of this dangerous technique.

In every sport, players should be taught the mechanisms of potential injury, the methods of avoiding and preventing such injuries, and constantly encouraged to employ a healthy attitude toward their athletic endeavor.

Injury Specialists

The employment of at least one certified athletic trainer in every institution or athletic organization is as necessary as the employment of a coach for every sport. Preferably, the athletic trainer should be on duty even during P.E. activity, but is particularly important during practice periods and games. The athletic trainer should have no responsibilities other than the health, safety, care, and treatment of the athletes. A regular program should be employed for the trainer to educate the coaches concerning problems and considerations of their particular sport, or involving a particular athlete.

Every team should likewise have a licensed medical practitioner with whom a fixed arrangement is made to render services as a team physician. This needs to be an individual capable of treating the whole body, rather than simply a specialized problem, and to whom the trainer and coaches can turn at any time for advice and care which is beyond the skill and expertise of the trainer. It is especially important that the team physician be present during games, since the rate and severity of injury are significantly greater there than during practice.

In addition to the team physician, who should probably be a general practitioner or one who specializes in family practice or sports medicine, the team should have access to specialists who might be called upon to handle more serious problems. At a minimum, these should include an orthopedic surgeon and a neurosurgeon, but there is wisdom in including an internist, a general surgeon and perhaps even a cardiovascular specialist. This may sound luxurious, but it involves no expenditure until an injury occurs. The point is to establish a relationship with particular physicians which is known to the athletic and medical personnel at the school, and to the physician and his/her staff. If a severe injury occurs, the school will know whom to call and the physician's office will know that it is a priority matter when the call is received. Many times the decision whether to contact a specialist will be made by the team physician, but his/her job is made easier if the school has undertaken the responsibility to establish satisfactory relationships with particular specialists.

Hospitals

The school should be aware of the facilities available at various hospitals, and particularly of those hospitals best equipped to handle serious emergency situations. For example, a "teaching hospital" which offers programs in orthopedic surgery and neurosurgery is preferable because at all times there is a specialist in the hospital. The school must assure that the injured athlete is taken to the correct facility and must notify the hospital of the athlete's impending arrival.

Teams which engage in contests against opponents in other towns must take additional special precautions to guarantee the availability of proper treatment in the event of injuries to their athletes. If the team physician cannot make such trips, the school must make arrangements for the attendance of a local physician at the game. The school must also have information concerning preferable hospital facilities and the names of specialists in advance of the contest so that there will be no time delay if an emergency should arise.

At all practices, as well as games, the equipment necessary for the handling of a serious emergency must be on the field. There must also be a telephone on the field to make an immediate call for help if it is needed. Every reasonable effort to reduce the delay in obtaining treatment for an injured athlete should be undertaken. Advance arrangements should be made for the fastest possible ambulance service to be available at both practices and games. Again, an important factor is the establishment of a relationship with the ambulance company so that they know to give the call a priority when it is received.

As pointed out by Russell Lane, M.D., team physician at Amherst College and a member of the NCAA Standing Committee on Competitive Safeguards and the Medical Aspects of Sports, "Our goals must be to have *good* athletic trainers, *good* medical back-up, *good* communications network, *good* available transportation, and a *good* hospital facility singled out as the ultimate destination. In short: a *good* plan for action."

Health and Safety

When an injury occurs, it must be given immediate attention and top priority. Far too often, the concern of a coach is to get the athlete back into action, or off the field so that play can continue, rather than determining the condition and needs of the victim. It is here, more than any other time, that the team needs the presence of someone whose sole concern is the care and treatment of injuries.

One of the gravest risks is the failure to consider and properly guard against those effects which are not immediately obvious. Such problems arise most commonly with respect to injuries to the neck, the cervical spine, the internal organs, the cardiovascular system, and as a result of excessive body heat. Injury to the head is often accompanied by an injury to the cervical spine, and vice versa.

A complete loss of sensation and/or motor function of a major portion of the body usually signifies trauma to the spinal cord, which should be carefully investigated. Although function and sensation return within a few minutes, there is a possibility of further movement of the vertebral column and permanent injury to the spinal cord.

Blows to the trunk may cause injury to the internal organs which requires immediate treatment. Athletes die of cardiac arrest which might have been avoided had coaches been more aware of, and paid more attention to the signs and symptoms leading to the cardiac failure. There is also an annual incidence of death from heat stroke which is completely avoidable.

Extreme caution should always be exercised in returning an athlete to action following an injury or illness. While there are obviously minor aches and pains which neither require nor justify medical examination, it is imperative that in every circumstance the coach consider the long-range well-being of the athlete rather than immediate concerns about expediting practice or winning a game.

Participation

In deciding whether an athlete should be allowed to participate, one of the most dangerous practices is to allow the athlete to make the decision. A variety of factors may lead athletes to insist upon continued participation when they are seriously injured. An excellent example is the recent experience of the Dallas Cowboys in a playoff game during which Roger Staubach suffered a serious concussion. After a lengthy medical examination, he reportedly returned to the field and informed coach Landry that he wanted to play, despite the fact that he was still suffering from substantial amnesia resulting from the concussion.

The preferable approach is to place all problems relating to the conditioning, training, and treatment of athletes in the hands of a trainer and physician. Realizing, however, that in many instances the school has not provided the athletic department with any medical assistance whatsoever, the foregoing information is designed to alert coaches to problem areas in which they should more thoroughly educate themselves, and also to caution them to take the most conservative approach in the interest of protecting athletes against injury, and also protecting the school against litigation.

V. A Capable Coach is the Best Defense against the Threat of Litigation

Competitive athletics has great potential for enhancing growth and development. This is best achieved by making sports as safe as possible. Theoretically, if this remains utmost in the minds of schools and coaches, they will need no further protection from litigation.

Unfortunately, litigation trends have created an added dimension for concern. For example, doctors must do more than give adequate, competent treatment; they must also employ special measures as precautions against malpractice suits. Similarly, the coach and school must go beyond protection of the athlete; they must also safeguard against litigation.

Two types of lawsuits pose a threat to school athletics. Indirectly, product liability cases against manufacturers and dealers of sporting goods have an impact upon school programs. Increases in insurance premiums are passed on to the schools through price increases. Football helmet manufacturers, for example, must charge between $3 and $15 per helmet just to cover liability insurance costs. Those figures could easily double or triple in the next 2-5 years. Of even greater concern are suits alleging negligence, the threat of which has directly increased.

Prudence of Coaches

To avoid liability for an injury, the school and coach must do no more than be "reason-ably prudent," in short, to be average—a "C-student." However, some "expert witness" may come forth in behalf of the injured party with an idealistic concept of what is reasonably prudent.

As unrealistic and impractical as these "20-20 hindsight" views may be, jurors are often persuaded to accept them. The results can be devastating. Last summer, a school district in California suffered a verdict of $1.2 million because a group of jurors were convinced that a tackling drill in which a player was injured was unreasonably dangerous.

Several areas of concern require attention to adequately protect the school. Some of these areas correlate closely with injury prevention. In general, coaches must attend carefully to equipment matters, teaching, training, and conditioning of athletes, and to medical care. They must also engage in effective public relations and wise handling of serious injury situations.

Standards and Helmets

In 1974, the National Operating Committee for Standards in Athletic Equipment (NOCSAE) published a standard for football helmets. The NCAA adopted a rule requiring that by September 1, 1978, all helmets in use by member schools had to meet that standard. The National Federation of State High School Associations extended its deadline for compliance to September 1, 1980.

In the view of the author, every school must immediately make all possible efforts to convert its football helmets to those which meet NOCSAE requirements. If a player suffers a brain injury in a non-certified helmet, strong argument will be made that the school was negligent in failing to meet a standard which it knew was designed to improve head protection. Absolute protection against injury is not possible, but no coach or school should provide its athletes with any less than the best equipment available.

Although no comparable standard has been developed for other types of protective equipment, it is foolishness to use equipment which does not meet the approval of recognized athletic organizations, or is significantly different in kind and quality from that recommended by respected leaders and experts in the particular sport.

Repair and maintenance of equipment must be consistent with the specifications of the manufacturer. Follow all instructions and use only those replacement parts intended for the equipment. Integration of parts from different manufacturers, permanent removal of parts or other substantial modification of the helmet, may not only be negligent, but also creates a new and different product for which the manufacturer may no longer be legally responsible.

Younger Players and Protection

Employ regular procedures for replacement of equipment. The practice of handing used equipment down to younger or less capable players must be undertaken with extreme caution. If protective capabilities have been reduced in the least, the equipment is no longer acceptable for *any* player.

No item of protective equipment is designed for indefinite use, and the fact that an item does not *appear* damaged is not always a dependable indicator. Prudence requires replacement every 3 to 4 years regardless of appearance. Once a decision is made to discard equipment, destroy it or completely transform it so no one can subsequently use it for protective purposes.

In the teaching of athletes, the first step is to instill an awareness of the risks of participation. Players need and have a right to know the mechanics of catastrophic injury, the limited capabilities of equipment, and the fact that some injury is inevitable. With this information, they will assume more responsibility for their own behavior, and be less likely to cast blame on others if an injury occurs.

Rules for Player Protection

Repeatedly emphasize the rules of the sport, particularly those designed for player protection. Give special attention to those rules designed to prevent severe injury (such as prohibitions against use of the head in football, or intentionally ramming into an opponent in baseball) by distributing written copies to every player. Teach athletes that violation of these rules most often results in injury to the violator and also requires them to relate back to the coach the substance of the rule and its purpose.

Take care to protect even against such unlikely occurrences as seizures, cramps, system arrest, or other physiologic dysfunction resulting from exertion when no adult is present to render aid. Lack of adequate supervision is probably the most common historic attack against school personnel; protect against all unsupervised activity.

Injury-prevention Clinics

Coaches must engage in a constant program of continuing education to keep themselves apprised of the latest information in training and conditioning. This requires not only academic study, but attendance at sports medicine and coaching clinics.

One very important source of information is the National Athletic Injury/Illness Reporting System (NAIRS). By enrolling in this program, a school receives regular reports regarding athletic injury and illness and their relationship to equipment, environment, and activity. With this information, schools and coaches can determine whether some controllable factor is creating a risk to athletes. To ignore the availability of such information would lead to serious problems if preventable injury or illness occurs. The use of such a program is one more indication that the school and coach are using every available means to protect athletes.

Training Personnel

In the area of medical attention, not enough emphasis can be given to the need for a certified athletic trainer. Today, there are not enough such people in the country to fill a job in every school. But until schools announce their willingness to hire trainers, there will be little incentive for interested people to pursue such a career. In the meantime, there are far more people available to engage in competent athletic training than there are positions available simply because schools have refused to recognize the need.

The argument that employment of a trainer is not economically possible will meet with harsh and unpleasant results in a lawsuit filed because an athlete was harmed by the absence of anyone qualified to deal with a serious injury. By expecting coaches to act as trainers, schools are exposing themselves to liability not only for the improper handling of an injury situation, but by failing to demonstrate total concern for the well-being of athletes. Every school must have on its staff a person whose sole concern is the health and safety of the athletes.

For schools where there is no trainer available, institute special measures for dealing with emergencies. The best alternative is a paramedic unit. The school must be certain that *immediately* upon the occurrence of injury a telephone is available and that all members of the athletic staff know where to call for help.

Likewise, it is the school's responsibility to be certain that the emergency aid agency is aware of the school's needs and of how to gain the fastest access to the injured athlete. Go to that agency before the school year with a map which shows the route to the school and the location of various facilities. It also would be wise to go through practice exercises with all members of the athletic staff and every potential ambulance driver. The school must make the decision where to take an injured athlete and give appropriate instructions rather than leaving that decision to an ambulance driver.

Returning Injured Athletes to Practice

In no instance should a coach make a medical decision to allow an athlete to return to activity after an injury or illness without medical advice. Obviously, occasions arise when even a layperson can determine that continued participation does not pose a hazard. But the absolute rule must be, "When in doubt, keep the athlete out."

Receipt of a consent or release form from a parent which allows return to activity is not adequate protection for the coach and school. Even when the physician has given clearance, the coach must be satisfied that the player is capable of tolerating every risk and stress which is to be expected from the activity.

Use of Effective Public Relations

One of the surest ways of generating a lawsuit arising out of an injury is for coaches to refuse to communicate effectively with the athletes and their parents, and to allow animosity to develop toward the program. It is not enough to engage in a public relations effort after the injury occurs; then, it may be too late. From the first day of practice, parents and athletes must know that the coach's door is always open, that they may express their discomforts, ask questions, or make suggestions.

Refusal to communicate may be interpreted as having something to hide; if tragedy strikes a family, they are much more likely to attack that kind of coaching situation.

It is an important safeguard against litigation that the athletic program maintain a highly visible profile in the community with repeated reminders of the valuable role it plays. If the program is respected and appreciated, thoughts of filing suit against it will be less likely to develop.

Careful attention must be given to the removal of every unnecessary or unreasonable risk from athletic programs. Many drills and techniques which were once accepted have been found to be dangerous.

Just as important to protection against litigation is elimination of anything which suggests that it is, or appears to be, unreasonably dangerous. One of the most common problems is vocabulary. Although phrases such as "suicide," "crucifixion," "hamburger," "meatgrinder," "gauntlet," and "punishment drill" have been used over the years, the response of parents of an injured athlete who was involved in such an exercise is something quite different. Use of such descriptive terms is certainly not essential to successful coaching.

At the start of every season, coaches should meet with the parents of athletes as a group to explain all that is being done to protect their children, from selection of the best equipment, to the use of extensive conditioning exercises to prepare all the athletes for participation.

Financial Burden

The strongest motivating factor for litigation is economic need. Families who suffer the tragedy of a catastrophic athletic injury are saddled with a horrendous financial burden. Inability to meet those demands causes parents to turn in desperation to lawyers and courtrooms. By providing a fund from which to care for the injured child, the school will reduce the risk of suit.

Schools must diligently search for the most extensive medical policy and then encourage parents to add a supplemental policy for their children who are involved in athletics. The author advocates that a specialized program which will provide both medical care and maintenance for life is an essential step to solving the litigation problem.

Should a tragic accident occur, the first and most important rule is, "Don't panic." The best example of creating litigation problems by overreacting emotionally to a tragedy is the "anguished doctor syndrome;" the physician who expresses grief for the death or poor result of a patient by exclaiming, "If only I had tried . . ." Most often, this is not an admission of error, but an expression of frustration with the outcome. However, it may come back to haunt the doctor in the courtroom.

Similarly, if a coach reacts to a case of quadriplegia by lamenting, "If only we had spent more time on tackling techniques," or,

"I wondered if she was ready to try that dismount technique," the words may someday be used against the coach and school in litigation.

The most dangerous practice following a severe injury is to speculate to anyone about why or how the tragedy occurred. Facts which were observed should be carefully recorded. Any possible evidence which might shed light on the situation must be carefully and permanently preserved. This includes the equipment involved, films or photographs of the occurrence, statements of witnesses, and the identity of all persons present who might be witnesses.

An immediate report and full cooperation must be given to the dealer and manufacturer of any equipment being used, and that equipment must be carefully stored away. It is especially important not to even remotely suggest fault or wrongdoing on the part of anyone else. Accusation of anyone may lead to litigation against everyone involved.

Full cooperation should be given to the representatives of the manufacturer, once assured that they will not ultimately attempt to blame the school or coach for the injury.

It is wise to obtain the advice and counsel of a lawyer, but this must be someone with particular expertise in athletic injury litigation.

Finally, the public relations effort referred to above must be renewed with fervor. Maintaining a good rapport with the athlete and family is crucial, but community relations are also important. The media can play a critical role in determining whether a suit will be filed. Reminders about the mechanisms of injury, the inability to absolutely prevent them, and the extensive safety measures employed in the school's program are essential.

Effective, widespread education and public relations is one of the solutions to the litigation problem. If coaches, athletes, and parents know how injuries occur, know that some cannot be prevented, but are convinced that the school and coach have done everything in their power to provide a safe experience, athletes will expend greater efforts to protect themselves, and parents will be less likely to employ a lawyer to solve their economic problems if an injury occurs. At every turn, coaches and schools must demonstrate that their supreme concern is for the health and safety of athletes.

In short, coaches must give as much attention to eliminating the risk of litigation as they give to producing a winning program.

Athletic Nutrition, Diet, and Weight Control 8

Kathy Heck, A.T.C.

Coaches, athletic trainers, and teachers are important information sources for athletes seeking nutritional advice. In providing such information two goals should be kept in mind: to assist the athlete in obtaining maximum performance through proper diet and weight control; to aid the individual in the development of good eating habits for later life.

Diet

There is no perfect athletic diet. In fact, the diet eaten by athletes should be just the same as for any normal individual—except for an increased caloric intake to provide sufficient energy for physical activity. The recommended "balanced diet" developed by the National Academy of Science's Food and Nutrition Board consists of:

Dairy Products
   2-4 servings daily
Fruits and Vegetables
   4 or more servings daily
Bread and Cereals
   4 or more servings daily
Meat, Fish, or Poultry
   2 or more servings daily

Protein

In addition to the basic four food groups, nutritionists have further identified six essential nutrients: proteins; fats; carbohydrates; vitamins; minerals; water. Actually eating the recommended servings of each of the basic food groups ensures the individual of getting all the essential nutrients except water.

Protein sources include meat, fish, dairy products, eggs, soybeans, etc. These foods are primarily utilized in the growth and repair of tissue and are only a secondary source of energy. Therefore, exercise does not greatly increase an athlete's daily protein requirement. A protein intake of one gram per two pounds of body weight per day is sufficient even when attempting to gain weight or strength during weight-training programs. To assure maximum utilization of protein, intake may be distributed throughout the day rather than ingesting the day's supply at a single meal.

Diets consisting of only protein foods may pose a hazard to the athlete. Excessive levels of protein intake may be toxic since the fixed acids of urea and ammonium are byproducts of protein metabolism. As waste products, these acids circulate in the body until filtered by the kidneys and excreted via the urine. Thus, an elevated level of waste products in circulation may contribute to early fatigue in the athlete. The high protein diet also requires that the individual's fluid intake be increased to assist the kidneys in filtering the fixed acids from the blood. Protein foods are slow to digest taking four to six hours to work their way through the stomach and upper bowel. For these reasons proteins are not the ideal element for pre-game meals in athletics. It is far more advantageous to replace the traditional steak and eggs with a high carbohydrate content meal.

Carbohydrates

Carbohydrates, the sugars and starches, compose the cereals and grains, e.g., waffles, spaghetti, breads, potatoes, etc. These foods provide the quickest and most efficient source of energy for athletic events. Carbohydrates are easily broken down to glucose and used for energy or converted to glycogen and stored in the liver and muscles. Glycogen storage is important to the athlete since it determines how long he or she can function prior to exhaustion. The average storage equals 1500-2000 calories. The depletion of stored glycogen is best illustrated by the phenomena of "hitting the wall" experienced by trained marathon runners. This is said to occur at the 20th mile of a marathon race, or after approximately two hours of time. After glycogen stores are depleted, the body must rely on energy stored in the form of fat.

By loading up on carbohydrates prior to competition, performance is not improved, but individuals may be able to maintain maximum exertion longer. This is of particular importance to athletes involved in endurance sports such as distance running, swimming, and cross-country skiing, soccer, field hockey, lacrosse, etc. The techniques of "carbohydrate loading" have been developed to assure maximum precompetition glycogen storage. The athlete begins seven days prior to competition and completes a workout similar to the length of the competitive event to deplete glycogen storage levels. For the next three days a high protein, low carbohydrate, diet is eaten and normal workouts are completed. Then, during the last three days prior to competition the athlete switches to a high carbohydrate, low protein diet, and the workouts are tapered. In this fashion, the athlete attempts to "load" glycogen prior to competition.

Obviously, the "carbohydrate loading" has disadvantages:

- Many athletes are unable to handle the toxic effects of high protein intake.
- The cycle takes a full week and cannot be done effectively more than several times per year.
- With an increase in glycogen storage, the athlete will also experience an accompanying increase in water storage (2.7 grams of water per gram of glycogen). This resulting increase in body weight may be detrimental to many athletes.
- The actual effects of the "carbohydrate loading" technique are questionable. Research on its effects is not conclusive, and proving that the positive effects are not merely psychological may be difficult.

For these reasons "carbohydrate loading" is not suggested for all athletes, particularly not for team sport athletes playing several games each week. But as a practical application, it is recommended that athletes in sports requiring a high level of endurance eat high carbohydrate content food in the last two to three meals prior to competition. This will ensure adequate levels of glycogen storage without encountering the undesirable side-effects of complete "carbohydrate loading."

Fats

When the body does consume all available glycogen stores, it switches to a more concentrated type of energy in the form of fat. As an energy source, fat provides twice as much energy per gram as do carbohydrates, but is a much more difficult substance to metabolize. It is thought that females are capable of metabolizing fat more easily than males, and this opens the possibility that female runners may have an advantage over males in ultra-distance races of 50 miles or more. Fats are necessary to the diet as sources of the fat-soluble vitamins A, D, E, and K and to provide satiety value and taste to foods. Dietary sources include oils, butter, animal fat, whole milk, fried foods, etc. Because high-fat content foods may be difficult to digest and slow the gastric emptying process, they should not be a major component of precompetition meals.

Vitamins

Vitamins are often a source of controversy in athletic nutrition. But despite the belief of many, there is no data to support the idea that performance is enhanced by vitamin supplementation. A well-balanced diet provides all of the necessary vitamins for athletes and non-athletes alike. Supplements to vitamins are recommended only if the daily diet is not of the proper composition. In that case a daily multiple vitamin supplement may be advised. Excessive intake of the fat-soluble vitamins (A, D, E, K) may be harmful since they are stored in the body and can build up to toxic levels. Excessive amounts of water-soluble vitamins (C and the B complex) are filtered through the kidneys and excreted via the urine on a continuous basis. Vitamin C, though when taken excessively, can be destroyed within the body and result in "rebound deficiency."

Minerals

Minerals of particular importance are iron, and the electrolytes involved in muscular contraction and relaxation, salt and potassium. Since anemia can be considered a stress injury attributed to heavy workouts, iron supplementation may be important to certain athletes. This may be particularly true for female athletes who lose iron on a monthly basis via menstruation. The electrolyte minerals are lost through perspiration and need to be adequately replaced to ensure maximum athletic performance. This can be achieved by salting food to taste and by regular dietary intake. When the athlete is undergoing extremely heavy workouts, electrolyte supplementation may be necessary, either by salt/potassium tablets or by commercial electrolyte preparations. Caution must be used in administering salt tablets to athletes. They should be taken only:

- with meals to avoid stomach upset;
- with a minimum of 8 ounces of water or other fluid to ensure proper water/salt concentration in the body;
- three to four hours prior to activity to allow salt to be present in the body during exercise.;
- at a rate of no more than one tablet per six pounds loss of body fluids; this is best determined by weighing prior to and following practice sessions.

Water

Water is an often-overlooked nutrient, but one that is of extreme importance in athletics. The normal individual requires a minimum of eight glasses (2000 ml) of fluids daily. This requirement is greatly increased for athletes because of fluids lost through perspiration, and dehydration can become a serious problem for athletes. Initially, it contributes to early fatigue and diminished performance, but dehydration can progress to muscle cramps, heat exhaustion, and even to the potentially fatal syndrome of heat stroke. Since adequate fluid intake is so important, unlimited access to water during workouts is essential. This is of particular importance in warmer climates and in sports where heavy protective equipment is worn. It has been found that the thirst mechanism is inadequate in assuring the body of proper fluid replacement. Therefore, it is useful to keep a daily weight chart to monitor fluid losses. The athlete should force fluids when the day's weight is not equal to the previous day's recorded weight. This can seriously affect performance, and the loss of one pound of body weight equals one pint of fluids.

Pre-game Meals

As previously mentioned, pre-game meals should consist of high-carbohydrate foods such as pancakes, waffles, spaghetti, macaroni, potatoes, breads, etc. The meal should be eaten three to four hours prior to gametime to assure the athlete of the smallest possible stomach volume. Fluids can comfortably be taken up to within 20-30 minutes before the start of activity. The pre-game meal should consist of foods familiar to the athlete and the meal should be nonirritating and pleasant-tasting. Milk has often been considered a poor pre-game beverage, but it may be very soothing to the athlete with a nervous stomach. Foods and beverages containing high concentrations of sugar should be avoided prior to and during competition. This includes candy bars, honey, and dextrose pills. High concentrations of sugar draw fluids to the gastrointestinal tract and slow gastric emptying. A solution as dilute as 2.5% glucose will decrease the rate of gastric emptying by 10%. Adequate blood sugar levels are important, but quantities ingested at a rate of greater than 50 grams (3 rounded tablespoons) per hour can impair performance. Rapidly consuming large amounts of sugar results in insulin being released to stabilize the blood sugar level. This results in a rapid decrease in the blood sugar level, and the body suffers a "roller coaster" effect which can lead to early fatigue and weakness.

Liquid meals may be useful for athletes, either as a dietary supplement for attempting to gain weight or as a pre-game meal. They may eliminate the dry mouth, abdominal cramps, and nausea experienced by athletes with pre-contest digestive distress. A liquid meal costs far less per serving than the traditional steak, and it can be a convenient way to feed athletes when playing away from home. There is no proof that liquid meals enhance athletic performance, but they do have advantages that make them useful in certain situations.

Weight Control

Since 20-30% of the American population is overweight, it is safe to assume that athletes are not immune from weight control difficulties. For athletes, excessive fat is dead weight that results in less speed, diminished endurance, and lower resistance to injury.

Height-weight charts are not always an accurate means of determining an athlete's ideal weight, especially the individual with a lot of muscle bulk. A better estimate is the body fat percentage which can be estimated by underwater weighing or skinfold calipers. It has been found that body fat percentage is inversely proportional to maximum oxygen uptake. In other words the athletes with lower body fat percentages seem to be those who can utilize oxygen most efficiently. The following chart indicates acceptable body fat percentages:

Sex	Athletes	Desirable	Obese
Male	7-12%	12-15%	20%+
Female	12-15%	15-25%	27%+

The key to weight control is that caloric expenditure must match or exceed caloric intake. To achieve this goal, the overweight athlete must undergo a permanent change in eating habits. One pound of weight gain results from the intake of 3,500 unused calories. An estimate of daily caloric requirements is as follows:

	Males	Females
To Maintain	2400	1900
To Lose	1500	1200
Light Activity	2900	2400
Moderate Activity	3700	3000
Heavy Activity	4300	3600

When attempting to lose weight, an athlete's intake should never drop below 1200 calories per day for females and 1500 calories for males. And weight loss should be gradual—no more than 2-3 pounds per week. Athletes should be especially encouraged to avoid fasting diets. Such rapid weight loss consists of only 35% fat and 65% lean body tissue. Therefore, this sort of diet is particularly dangerous for athletes and growing adolescents. Sensible eating is important to any weight control program. Obviously, if fad diets worked, the constant flow of new ones would not exist. Most are dangerous, ineffective, and boring. It should be a matter of year-round concern; "starving down" in pre-season is unwise and unhealthy.

Summary

There are no wonder foods or winning dietary formulas for the athlete. The basics of nutrition are as important as the basic skills of the sport itself. Only through proper diet and weight control can the athlete achieve his or her full potential and develop good eating habits for the future.

Coping with the Heat and Humidity 9

Holly Wilson, A.T.C., Ph.D.

With the beginning of either the fall or spring sports season, the coach should be concerned with environmental conditions of heat and humidity, particularly in the midwest and southern regions of the United States. While a hot environment poses a threat to the active athlete it is not as dangerous as one in which the humidity level is also high. In a hot, humid environment the active athlete may be unable to maintain the core temperature of the body within its narrow critical range of 96-108°F.

The athlete is not only generating body heat through activity but also absorbs heat from the environment when the atmospheric temperature is greater than that of the skin's surface. The major temperature regulatory mechanism of the body is sweating; however, as the humidity level increases, indicating that the atmosphere is approaching saturation, cooling through sweating becomes ineffective. Sweat must evaporate for cooling to take place. In a hot, humid environment when evaporation of sweat is hindered, the athlete continues to sweat and this is when the individual may get into trouble.

Weight loss during activity is primarily fluid loss, not the metabolism of fat. For example, if the athlete runs at a rate of 5 mph, 7.5 cal/kg of body weight/hour would be expended. Therefore, an athlete weighing 60 kg (132 pounds) would expend only 450 calories if the individual ran for one hour without stopping at a rate of 5 mph. One pound equals 3500 calories. For every two pounds of body weight the athlete loses during activity, one quart of water has been lost. This fluid comes from the body fluids so the circulatory blood volume decreases as the athlete continues to sweat. Heat stress is an embarrassment of the circulatory system.

If the athlete loses only 1% of the body weight (1.3 pounds in a 132-pound athlete) due to water loss, there is some physiological impairment—reflex time decreases as does strength. Under such a condition, the athlete may be more susceptible to injury because the individual is unable to react as quickly or exert as much force. Of course, the athlete's susceptability to injury would increase as fluid continues to be lost. At a 3% loss of body weight (approximately 4 pounds in a 132-pound athlete) pulse rate increases as does rectal temperature. The reflex response continues to decrease and the athlete becomes less mentally alert. The athlete becomes susceptible to heat exhaustion as a 6% loss of body weight is approached; however, a gray area is entered with a weight loss of 3-6%. Some athletes will show signs of heat exhaustion while in this gray area due to individual differences. The signs and symptoms of heat exhaustion are:

- pale, clammy skin;
- increase in respiratory rate;
- muscular weakness;
- decrease in blood pressure;
- normal or subnormal body temperature;
- nausea and vomiting.

The increased respiratory rate and vomiting compound the problem even more because both result in additional fluid loss. The athlete displaying symptoms of heat exhaustion should be removed from activity, taken to a cooler area, wet clothing removed if possible, and fluids administered. The athlete may be a candidate for heat stroke, if fluid balance is not restored. It is important to force fluids for thirst is not a good indicator of the athlete's fluid needs.

The athlete is susceptible to heat stroke when more than 6% of the body weight is lost (approximately 8 pounds, in a 132-

pound athlete). The signs and symptoms of heat stroke are lethargy, lightheadedness, dizziness, confusion, vomiting, diarrhea, muscle cramps, unconsciousness, and an elevated body temperature. In addition, the athlete has hot dry skin because the sweating mechanism has turned off. The individual has lost all the fluid the body can spare through sweating in an attempt to regulate body temperature. (The critical temperature at which brain damage occurs is 108°F.) Every attempt must be made to reduce the athlete's temperature as quickly as possible, or death may occur. The athlete may be placed on a chair under a cold shower, submerged in a cold whirlpool, sponged off with lukewarm water (not alcohol) or cooled with an electric fan. Call a physician and ambulance immediately because, in most cases, the athlete is unable to take fluids orally so they must be administered intravenously.

Watch the tall lean participant closely in a hot humid environment. This individual produces more heat per body area than the overweight individual who is carrying excess metabolically inactive tissue, fat. However, the latter individual does expend additional energy lugging around the excess weight.

To prevent heat stress, acclimatize athletes to the environmental conditions in which they are going to be active. Acclimatization varies according to the time of year, the geographical location, and the sports activity. Athletes must be conditioned to the temperature, the humidity, and even the clothing which they are going to wear during participation. The physical condition of each athlete at the beginning of the season is a major contributing factor in susceptibility to heat stress. The conditioned athlete conserves body salts (electrolytes) by producing a less-concentrated sweat and sweating less profusely. Each athlete should engage in an individualized off-season conditioning program so he/she can return to school in good, if not excellent, physical condition.

The athlete should begin the conditioning program approximately eight weeks prior to the season. The program should focus on the development of cardiorespiratory fitness, both aerobic and anaerobic. The amount of participation in each will be determined by the sport in which the athlete is going to compete. Suggested activities for developing cardiorespiratory fitness are running, swimming, and bicycling. In addition, the athlete should not ignore the development of strength through weight-training. Cardiorespiratory fitness activities should be scheduled three days a week and weight-training two days a week.

The athlete should be active at approximately the same time that practice will be scheduled in the fall or spring. Only in this way will the individual become acclimatized to the heat and humidity. The athlete should wear clothing similar to the school's athletic uniform in both fiber content and body area covered.

In the fall or spring, early season practices must be progressive to achieve acclimatization. Alternate work and rest periods, but do not drag out practices. Make them short and hard. Provide plenty of water and allow the athlete to take water breaks when desired, and not according to the coaches' schedules. Do *not* give salt tablets or a saline solution prior to or during activity. The high concentration of salt in the gastrointestinal tract, as a result of ingesting salt tablets or a hypertonic saline solution (greater than 0.9%), requires dilution before absorption can occur. Consequently, fluid is withdrawn from the body fluids to dilute the salt. A hypotonic solution (0.1%) may be used *after* practice to replace the fluid lost during activity; however, salting of food regularly will usually replace the salt lost in the sweat. The same holds true for potassium supplementation especially if fresh fruits or vegetables are regularly eaten. Items high in potassium but low in calories include oranges, grapefruits, apricots, watermelons, cantaloupes, tomatoes, artichokes, and brussels sprouts. Avocadoes, bananas, dates, and raisins are good sources of potassium but they are also high in calories. Replacement of fluid is the critical thing!

Instead of purchasing a commercial saline solution, which tends to be expensive, you may make your own with 6 quarts of water, 1 teaspoon of salt, and a flavoring. This is a 0.1% saline solution that can be absorbed without further dilution in the gastrointestinal tract. Do not use a flavoring that requires the addition of sugar for sweetening. Sugar increases the emptying time of the stomach and may cause intestinal cramping and diarrhea.

Make use of a weight chart to ensure that the athletes are not losing too much fluid and approaching chronic dehydration. (See Table 1.) Weigh each athlete before practice and then immediately after, before the individual has ingested any water (other than that during practice). Repeat this procedure every day. Each athlete should weigh in (before practice) at approximately the same

Table 1. Weight chart.*

*Reprinted with the permission of Cramer Products, Inc.

Date	Time of Practice	Rel. Humidity Wet Bulb Temp.	Name of Player				
			Before				
			After				
			Wt. Loss				
			Before				
			After				
			Wt. Loss				
			Before				
			After				
			Wt. Loss				
			⋮				
			Before				
			After				
			Wt. Loss				

weight every day. An athlete with a water loss problem, should be watched closely. The individual should prehydrate by drinking 1-3 quarts of fluid prior to each practice, spreading the intake out over several hours.

If an athlete is unable to regain fluid balance between practices the individual is more susceptible to heat stress and may become chronically dehydrated. The signs of chronic dehydration are loss of appetite, nausea, and diarrhea as well as the loss of weight. Prehydration is a necessity with this athlete; otherwise dehydration will affect vital body processes. For example, if the athlete does not have enough fluid the kidneys cannot adequately remove the waste products of exertion. In effect, the blood becomes too thick to pass through the kidney tubules for cleansing. Consequently, the athlete may develop a subclinical uremia. For adequate kidney clearance the athlete should excrete 1000 to 1500 cc of urine per day. Even with prehydration, if the athlete does not regain body weight, the individual should be withheld from practice and examined. There may be a reason other than fluid loss for continued weight loss. Usually it is an improper diet.

The intensity of each practice should be determined by the environmental conditions, not the coach. Immediately before practice, check the temperature and humidity by calling the local radio or weather station. The following chart should be a guide as to the intensity of practice.

Temperature	Humidity	Activity
80-90° F	Under 70%	O.K.
80-90° F	Over 70%	Caution, rest (particularly during early season).
90-100° F	Under 70%	Caution, rest.
90-100° F	Over 70%	Shorten practice or change time.
Over 100°		Shorten practice or change time.

As a rule of thumb, anytime the temperature and humidity levels add up to 150 or more, curtail the practice, change the practice time, or schedule a "chalk talk." By taking a few simple precautions heat stress can be guarded against and hopefully many problems eliminated.

Emergency Preparation* 10

Holly Wilson, A.T.C., Ph.D.

To borrow a well-known phrase, *be prepared*, before an emergency occurs. A predetermined emergency plan should be established and frequently reviewed so that everyone involved knows and understands what to do when and if an emergency does occur.

Field Set-up

The activity area should be set up prior to every practice and game to deal with the care of common injuries. Accept the fact that injuries are part of the game, but those injuries that do occur may not seem as disruptive of psyche, practice, or the game plan, if prepared. Chance of injury can frequently be minimized by making a daily inspection of the playing surface and surrounding area. Check fields for holes and debris such as glass, metal, and empty cans. In the gym, loose boards, wet spots on the floor, nearby windows, and wall fixtures that project outward are just a few of the many hazards that may need to be contended with. Equipment stored around the edges of the court is usually forgotten about but could also be a potential hazard.

Water, ice packs, towels, a blanket, splints, an arm sling or a triangular bandage, and a first aid kit should be on the sidelines for immediate use every time the team takes the field or court for a practice or game whether it be at home or away. Water may be stored in a cooler or in plastic squirt bottles if a hose or drinking fountain is not nearby. A high impact plastic cooler is superior to the styrofoam type. Although more expensive, the additional cost is soon justified by its longevity. Plastic coolers are available in 2-, 3-, and 5-gallon sizes. Squirt bottles are not as hygienic as paper cups but ease and economy often "justify" their use. They are easier

to carry and store if housed in a wire or wooden rack. Unfortunately, the plastic-coated cardboard carrier in which many manufacturers pack a set of six bottles quickly deteriorates. A student in a woodshop class can make a rack without much difficulty. Throughout the activity period, the water supply should be frequently checked. Water should be available to the athletes according to individual need, not the coach's schedule. Provide ice, water, paper cups, and towels for the visiting team if at all possible.

Any of the splints commercially-available (board, plastic air, cardboard, or ladder), is suitable for sideline use. (See Figure 1.) Some splints come arranged in sets packaged in handy carrying kits. Keep in mind, however, a suspected fracture should only be splinted by someone knowledgeable in proper splinting techniques as well as the use of the particular splint. A simple non-angulated fracture could become a more serious injury and possibly an open fracture (one with an external wound) when handled roughly or improperly.

It is highly recommended that all coaches complete a course in advanced first aid and emergency care offered by a local chapter of the American Red Cross.

First Aid Athletic Training Kit

The first aid athletic training kit need not be an expensive medical bag, athletic training kit, or compartmentalized paramedic case. A simple tool box or fishing tackle box is a satisfactory substitute. In the latter instance, however, one or more of the plastic

---

*The copyright for this article has been retained by the author. Similar material will appear in a book, *Coaches' Guide to Athletic Injuries*, which has been accepted for publication by Human Kinetics Publishers.

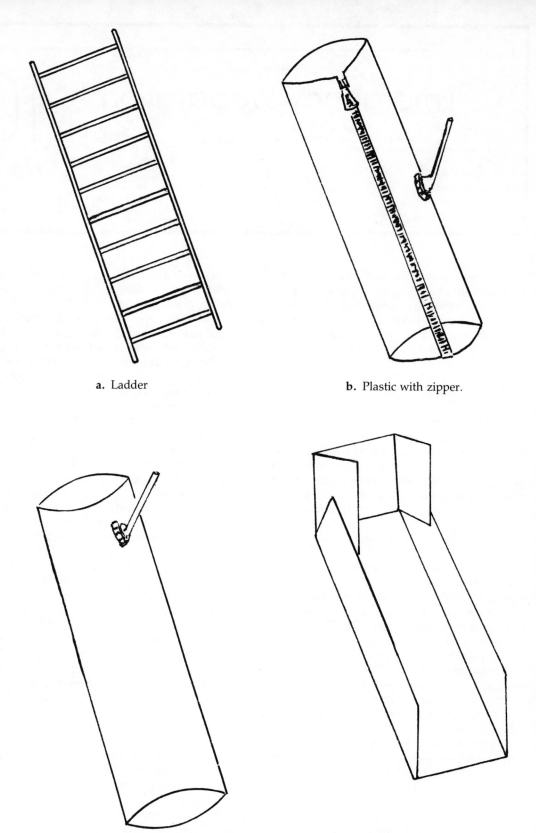

a. Ladder

b. Plastic with zipper.

c. Plastic without zipper.

d. Cardboard.

Figure 1. Commercially-available splints.

trays may need to be removed (simply cut through the rivets with a metal saw). Ideally the case should be tall enough so that bottles and spray cans can be stored upright. Do not buy a prestocked athletic training kit for many of the items are seldom used.

The kit should be checked after each practice and game and, if necessary, restocked. Only the person delegated to care for injuries should use the items in the kit. Only with such a restriction do the contents remain in order and readily available in adequate amounts. A well-equipped first aid athletic training kit should contain the following items:

- Elastic Bandage (cotton)*—at least one 3-inch, one 4-inch, and one 6-inch bandage should be packed; if there is room, pack another 4-inch bandage.
- Tape*—carry 2-3 rolls of 1½-inch athletic tape. It can easily be split to the desired width. Add more if needed and if space is available.
- Tape Adherent—it is more economical to paint the involved area with liquid than to use an aerosol spray. The liquid must be stored in an airtight container so that the ingredients do not evaporate. Apply a lubricant such as petroleum jelly around the rim of the jar and the lid for ease in removal. A regular paint brush may be used for application of the adherent. After using the brush, clean it with tape remover. Recently, a pump spray applicator for tape adherent was introduced on the market as an economical alternative to the aerosol spray. Similar containers may be found at a local hardware store. It may be necessary to clean the nozzle frequently to prevent the adherent from plugging up.
- Tape Remover—instead of the liquid, a box of single, individually packaged gauze pads saturated with tape remover can be purchased. In the long run, these unit dose packages may be more economical and are certainly less messy and easier to use. Make sure the athlete thoroughly washes the skin with soap and water after using any tape remover.
- Underwrap—pack one roll unless a lot of taping is done. (If so, critically examine whether all the taping needs to be done.)
- Tape Cutter—if possible always use a tape cutter to cut off a strapping. Cutting through many thicknesses of tape quickly makes bandage scissors dull.
- Bandage Scissors*—stainless steel scissors are more expensive than chrome and there is little justification for the added expense. The standard size scissors used in the training room are 7¼ inches; however, 5½-inch ones are useful when cutting bandages off small body parts. Scissors might be available at a very nominal cost from government surplus.
- Nail Clippers
- Tweezers*—splinter forceps available from a medical supply dealer are more useful than the tweezers found in most drug stores. Once again, chrome is fine.
- Penlight Flashlight*
- Antiseptic Cleansing Agent*—although it is a poor antiseptic, 3% hydrogen peroxide is recommended because its foaming action may loosen embedded debris. Store it in a light resistant amber bottle so that the hydrogen peroxide does not break down into its component parts.
- Mild Soap*—do not use an antibacterial or deodorant soap for cleansing wounds. Instead, use a mild soap such as Ivory or Camay.
- Antiseptic Solution—Isopropyl alcohol or one of the nonstaining, nonstinging iodine derivatives (povidone-iodine) such as Betadine is recommended.** The latter is more expensive.
  Frequently, either one of these two antiseptics is used to disinfect a "tool" such as a pair of splinter forceps prior to use.
- Antiseptic Cream*—carry a mild, single ingredient cream. An ointment has a greasy base that seals off the wound and may make it more prone to infection.
- Skin Lubricant—petroleum jelly is perhaps the most common and available lubricant used in the training room.
- Sterile Gauze Pads*—3 × 3-inch pads are the most useful size; however 4 × 4-inch pads may be needed to cover larger wounds. Cut smaller sizes from the larger pads, but keep each pad in the protective wrapper while cutting. If taping only a few ankles, use 3 × 3-inch

---

*Recommended for preparation of a first aid kit only.

**Most of the microorganisms that enter a wound are washed away with a thorough soap and water cleansing and those culprits that do remain are easily handled by the body's natural defenses. Surface wounds are usually better off without any one of the many antiseptics found on the drug store shelves. (Deep wounds should be left for the physician.) If an antiseptic must be used, apply it to the edges of the wound and surrounding area, not the open skin, especially if using Isopropyl alcohol!

pads to protect the heel and lace areas. Otherwise, it is more economical to use nonsterile gauze sponges or "bubbles," 3 × 3-inch squares cut from sheets of air bubble packing material.

- Bandaids*—if economically feasible, carry all three strip sizes, 1 × 3-inch strips, 3/4 × 3-inch strips, and extra large. If the budget is limited, omit the 3/4-inch (the one-inch strip can be cut down to the desired width). Purchase bandaids in boxes of 100 or an industrial pack to save money.
- Butterfly Closures or Steri Strips— butterfly closures are useful to temporarily close lacerations. Although commercially-available, a butterfly can easily be made from a small strip of athletic tape. (See Figure 2.) Steri Strips are often used by physicians to close a laceration instead of stitching the wound. They are expensive and available only in boxes of 100 packets, each packet containing several strips depending on the width. The 1/8-inch or 1/4-inch width is most frequently used. Perhaps a local physician would donate a packet or two as well as give instructions on the proper use and application of such closures.
- Gauze Bandages*—conforming, self-adhering bandages are easier to use than plain gauze bandages but are more expensive. Carry a few 2-inch rolls.

- Analgesic Balm—a water-soluble analgesic is recommended instead of an oil base one. Regardless, the balm should be mild, especially if used for analgesic packs.
- Tongue Depressors—besides being used as ointment spreaders, the junior size depressors double as temporary finger splints. (For injuries to the first or second segment, bend the depressor so it is curved; otherwise, for injuries to the third segment, leave the depressor straight. Regardless, pad the splint before applying it to the injured finger.)
- Cotton-tipped Applicators (Sterile)*— store the cotton-tipped applicators and tongue depressors in a closed container to retain their cleanliness. Some toothbrush holders work well.
- Hand Mirror—a protective case may be made from felt.
- Eyewash (Sterile)—avoid using a product containing boric acid. Boric acid is potentially dangerous because, in some cases, it has been found to be a systemic poison.
- Contact Lens Wetting Solution (Sterile)—different solutions are required for hard and soft lenses.
- Contact Lens Storage Case—many opticians specializing in contact lens care have extra plastic cases in which lenses

---

*Recommended for preparation of a first aid kit only.

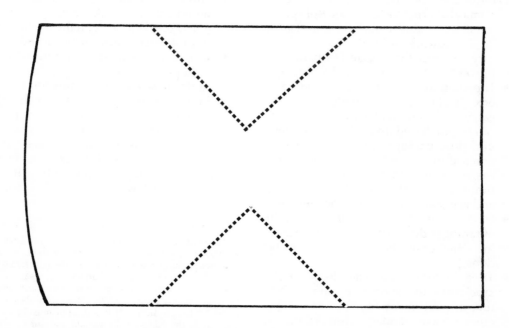

Figure 2. Pattern for making a butterfly closure.

are shipped. If necessary, use these for *temporary* storage of lenses.

- Towel Squares, Disposable Baby Diapers, or Combine—for making analgesic packs.
- Adhesive Felt and Foam—1/8- and 1/4-inch thicknesses are the most useful for making donuts and other speciality pads.
- Moleskin
- Vinyl Foam—1/4- and 3/8-inch thicknesses are used for padding bruises (contusions) and tender areas.
- Triangular Bandage or Sling*
- Safety Pins†
- Rubber Bands†
- Needle and Thread†
- Tampons—be alert to the early warning signs of Toxic Shock Syndrome—a high fever (usually 102° F or higher), vomiting or diarrhea, and a rash that looks like sunburn. Avoid brands that incorporate a deodorant into the tampon.
- Aspirin—purchase a small quantity of a good house brand. However, there may be restrictions from dispensing medication by the regulations of the school board.
- Change for a Telephone Call*
- List of Emergency Phone Numbers*
- First Aid Manual*
- First Aid Policies and Procedures*

It may be necessary to pack two kits. One should contain the materials required for strapping and padding while the other is solely for first aid care. A zippered vinyl gym bag is suitable for the strapping and padding supplies.

If possible, supplies should be bought locally at the drug store, medical supply company, or a sporting goods store. It may be necessary to purchase supplies from several places for a preference may develop for certain brand items. Frequently, local business people are more than willing to donate supplies to help a team out. For example, a local pharmacist may donate new empty prescription bottles and capsules to use as containers in the first aid athletic training kit. (Be sure that every item in the kit is well-labeled: name of the product; directions for use; precautions; expiration date.) In addition, manufacturers of over-the-counter products often send pharmacists unit dose or trial size samples of new products. Some of the products may be suitable for the care of athletic injuries. A local camera shop may donate empty plastic film canisters or plastic slide boxes. Both are useful containers for the first aid athletic training kit.

A few money-saving tips are listed below. Undoubtedly some additional ideas may arise as a result of a limited budget.

1. Ice may be available for first aid use from a nearby concession stand or cafeteria. Buy a bag of ice if necessary rather than using commercially-made chemical cold packs. The chemical cold packs are expensive and they do not get as cold or last as long as ice packs. If they leak, the chemical may cause irritation to the skin, especially if a wound is present. Aerosol cold sprays are dangerous (frostbite) and absolutely unnecessary! Plastic bags and ice will suffice for all needs. A local grocery store may donate a roll of plastic bags used in the fruit and vegetable section. If bags must be purchased, the heavy duty plastic bags with the ziplock closure may be more expensive but they outlast flimsier bags. The zip closure makes it easy to pour out water as ice melts.
2. Cups for ice massage may be reused. Put a tongue depressor or spoon in the water before freezing and use it as a handle during application. If available, small metal juice cans are ideal containers for freezing.
3. Warm wet towels or hot water bottles can be used as a superficial heat modality in place of a heat pack. A 15-20-minute hot shower with the shower head aimed at the injured part may also be therapeutic; but only if swelling is controlled.
4. A hose and a large plastic container can be used to simulate a whirlpool. When treating a new injury, do not direct the flow of the cold water against the tender tissue. The force of the water can aggravate the sensitive area and result in an increase in swelling.
5. Plain aerosol shaving cream may be used in place of mild soap for cleansing wounds. Although slightly more expensive, the shaving cream is easier to use.
6. Old socks may be used as ice packs. Fill the sock with ice and tape the end

---

*Recommended for preparation of a first aid kit only.

†These loose items may be carried in a plastic container such as a soap box along with nail clippers, splinter forceps, and mirror.

shut. Store the sock dry in the freezer or cooler. Just before use, moisten the sock with water and then place it on the injury.

7. Gauze sponges rather than sterile gauze pads or cottonballs can be used for cleanups such as removing tape adherent and tape residue. The sponges are not sterile so they should not be used to clean wounds.

8. An applicator for liquid tape adherent can be made from a tongue depressor and a piece of felt. Staple the felt to the end of the depressor.

9. A convenient container for carrying gauze pads in the first aid kit can be made from the bottom half of a large rectangular plastic medication bottle. Ask a local pharmacist to save empty bottles and then cut off the upper half with a warm sharp knife. Tape the cut edge.

10. Heavy duty plastic bags with a ziplock can be used in the first aid kit to keep items together, clean, and waterproof.

11. Used elastic bandages may be available from a local hospital. Check with the emergency room or orthopedic department because used bandages are frequently discarded.

12. Plastic cores from tape rolls can be trimmed into a protective covering for an injury to the fingernail or toenail. Pad the inner surface with adhesive foam or a sterile gauze pad.

13. A plastic bottle rack makes an ideal tray for serving water to a team. If the slots are labeled with each player's name then the same paper cup may be repeatedly used by the player so cups can be conserved. Replace the cups everyday for each practice and game.

Emergency Plan

Even if the proper emergency equipment and supplies are readily accessible on the sidelines, prompt action is impossible without a predetermined plan for handling emergencies. The plan should be developed long before the beginning of the season and it should be evaluated frequently and changed as necessary. After all, different sports practice at different sites, so some modification in the plan is required with the change of seasons. Personnel from the local ambulance service, the team physician, the trainer, the school principal, and the coach-ing staff should all have input in the development of the plan.

Responbibilities must be delegated according to each individual's capabilities. To execute the plan quickly and efficiently, each person must know the task assigned to them and understand just what is involved to carry out the task. Pinpoint critical locations beforehand. For example, where is the nearest entrance to the field that is accessible to an ambulance? If it is a locked gate, will it be unlocked during practices and games, or will the key be readily accessible? Where is the nearest phone? If only a pay phone is nearby, the appropriate change must be readily available. Tape the coins to the inside of the first aid kit along with a list of all the emergency phone numbers. Include on the list the numbers for the local ambulance or rescue squad, hospital emergency room, fire department, police department, team physician, school health center, school principal, etc. Also include the names and numbers of those medical specialists who have worked with the team. When working with minors, carry an emergency care card on each athlete. Emergency care cards should include the following information:

- the name and phone number, home and business, of parents or guardian;
- the name and phone number of the family physician;
- information on allergies and medical problems such as asthma, epilepsy, diabetes, etc.;
- faith, religion;
- a record of injuries incurred by the athlete and the corresponding treatments.

Telephone calls should be made only by the designated individual. If in a school setting, there may be a set protocol to follow. For example, the school district may have a contract with one of the local ambulance companies for athletic events. Check with the school principal or school board to be sure that the emergency plan complies with any established protocol.

In an emergency, while the designated individuals give first aid, call the ambulance or rescue squad, the parents or guardian, and the family and/or team physician. When talking with the ambulance service, give your name and role, the type of injury (head, neck, spine, extremity, internal), and the exact location of the injured athlete. *Also inform the service of the number of the phone from which the call is being made. Do not hang up first for the service may not have all the required in-*

formation. Remain at the phone to provide any additional information or clarify any facts if the service calls back. If the directions to the location are complicated and an extra person is available, ask the individual to meet the ambulance at the point where driving is no longer possible, or directions become confusing. The individual can then direct the ambulance or rescue squad to the injured athlete. If possible, prior to the season, review with the ambulance service personnel the location of the various playing fields and courts and the best access to each.

With little planning and effort, the athletic environment can be made safer. Such precautions are well worth the time and effort if only one injury can be prevented. It is not enough to have a predetermined plan; it must be understood, practiced by all, evaluated frequently, and modified as necessary. Furthermore, all coaches should be knowledgeable not only about the skills of the sport, but first aid and CPR techniques as well.

Legal Liability

It is well worth the time to become familiar with the laws of the state regarding the care of an injury victim whether employed fulltime, paid coach, or unpaid volunteer.‡‡. Many states have a Good Samaritan Law that protects the individual who stops to provide aid to a stricken individual. To be protected under this law, however, care must be provided that would be equivalent to that given by others with similar backgrounds in a similar situation. A coach or physical education teacher has a responsibility to students or athletes to provide a higher standard of care than a member of the general public. Both the coach and the physical education teacher should have received specialized training in first aid.

First aid techniques are recognized by the court as being the accepted standard of care to be used in an emergency. There is a big difference between first aid and treatment. As a first aider, recognize and understand this difference. The best safeguard is to know personal limitations and provide care accordingly. Let common sense be the guide.

Neither a waiver nor the fact that a coach might not be paid for services protects him/her from possible liability in the event of an injury. The court does not recognize waiver forms for minors because parents cannot sign away the rights of a minor, even when the individual is their offspring. Moreover, whether paid or not, the coach is responsible for the group and must perform competently at his/her level of training.

To be protected as a coach, against a lawsuit, and more importantly, to protect the welfare of athletes, take these precautions:

- Develop a sense of safety awareness and incorporate it in the philosophy of sport just as if it were part of the strategy of the game.
- Maintain equipment and facilities through periodic inspection and repair. Both should be thoroughly checked before activity. Facilities should be planned and their use scheduled to avoid over-crowding.
- Require annual medical examinations for all athletes. Such exams should be scheduled before the beginning of the season, early enough to allow for possible remediation of any problems uncovered during the testing. However, the time period should not be so long that an athlete could be injured before practice starts. The medical staff performing the examinations should have the final say concerning each athlete's clearance to participate. Recommendations for rehabilitation of specified individuals must be carried out before permission is granted to practice. (Agency-sponsored programs such as Little League Baseball or Pop Warner Football should also require a signed physical examination form from the family physician each year.)
- Keep up to date on the techniques and strategies of particular sport(s). Be responsible and teach athletes how to avoid injuries and how to perform in the sport. This involves teaching proper techniques as well as appropriate use and care of protective equipment, precautions for weather extremes, and the risks of competing when ill, injured, or not fully recovered from an injury. Proper preparation as a coach includes training in first aid techniques (at least a course in Standard First Aid and Cardiopulmonary Resuscitation.) A course in Advanced First Aid and Emergency Care is highly recommended. All three courses are frequently offered by the

---

‡‡Taking this one step further, look into the state laws concerning the operation of physical therapy modalities. If employed at a school where various treatment modalities are made available to coaches (and athletes), be prepared for a surprise! In many states only physical therapists working under the supervision of a physician can legally operate such modalities.

American Red Cross. If possible, complete courses in child growth and development, anatomy, and physiology.

- Schedule competition based on size, weight, and skill level of the participants rather than age or grade level. Individuals should not be forced into competition until physically and mentally prepared. Equipment fitting should take into account size, strength, and skill of the participant. Officials should be competent so that the intensity of the game can be controlled.
- Arrange with a local physician or group of physicians to provide medical coverage for all games and practices. If the physician designated as the team physician cannot be in attendance at all games, arrangements must be made with another physician to cover the event(s). (If permitted by league rules, a certified athletic trainer could cover the game(s) in place of a physician.) For practices, it may be possible to secure the services of an emergency medical technician or paramedic.
- Work closely with the physician and other coaches and allied health personnel before the season begins to develop first aid policies and procedures for the care and disposition of an injured athlete. Make sure that all coaches receive a copy of the policies and procedures and that a copy is included in each first aid athletic training kit. Review them periodically during the season.
- Allow sufficient time for conditioning prior to the beginning of the competitive season. Time must also be permitted for the teaching, learning, and practicing of new skills. During each practice, schedule sufficient time for warm-up, cool-down, and water breaks.

Regardless of the precautions taken, injuries do occur. In some instances, it may be difficult to determine whether the injury is serious enough to take the athlete out of activity. While it is easy to distinguish between a mild and severe injury, the difference between a mild and moderate one may be more perplexing. When in doubt, lean toward conservatism. Treat the injury as the more serious one. Think in terms of a long-range goal, the well-being of the athlete. The starter going at half speed with an injury may not be as good as the second or third stringer going at full speed. Educate athletes about the risks of participating when ill or injured. No athlete who has been withheld from activity as a result of an injury or illness should be permitted to return to practice and/or competition without medical clearance. If such clearance is not obtained before allowing the athlete to participate, the coach is legally liable if the athlete is reinjured or sustains another injury as a result of the disabled condition.

Report all injuries. Information gathered from these reports is invaluable in identifying causes. It also implements the development of more effective safety precautions. To be useful, injury reports should be filled out completely and should include the following information:

- time, date, place, activity;
- name and address of injured individual;
- description of injury;
- mechanism of injury (how it occurred);
- complaint (the part injured, symptoms);
- first aid rendered;
- medical diagnosis and disposition;
- nature and date of medical clearance for return to practice;
- restrictions;
- date of medical clearance for unlimited return;
- name, address, and phone number of witnesses (2);
- name and signature of individual making report.

The last four items of information cannot be recorded until after the athlete is examined by a physician and released for activity. Keep the completed reports on file for ready reference if the need arises.

Everyone involved in athletics should have personal liability insurance. In addition, if working directly with the athletes, everyone should have a thorough understanding of the insurance coverage provided by the school or league. It might also be wise to check the insurance policy on the car used to transport athletes. Coverage of this may not be included in personal insurance.

This form will be kept confidential and will be used as supplementary information by the examining physician.

Date of Physical_____

Name _____ **Age**_____ **Height** _____ **Weight** _____
      last   first

Birthdate _____ **Social Security or I.D.#** _____

School Address _____ **Phone** _____

Parent or Guardian _____

Home Address _____ **City** _____ **State** _____ **Phone** _____

I am a candidate for the _____ **Team**
                                    sport

Medical History (circle and/or check appropriate answer):

1. Have you ever been treated for any of the following:

    Yes   No   infectious mononucleosis
    Yes   No   virus pneumonia
    Yes   No   asthma
    Yes   No   rheumatic fever
    Yes   No   scarlet fever
    Yes   No   heart murmur
    Yes   No   epileptic seizure
    Yes   No   hepatitis
    Yes   No   diabetes
    Yes   No   sickle cell anemia
    Yes   No   illness requiring rest over one week
                    during the past year

2. If answer is "yes" to any of the above, please provide dates and treatment received for the illness.

    _____

    _____

3. During the past five (5) years have you received any of the following injuries:

    Yes   No   knocked out
    Yes   No   concussion
    Yes   No   severe headaches
    Yes   No   whiplash
    Yes   No   pinched nerve
    Yes   No   fracture of head or neck
    Yes   No   sprained neck
    Yes   No   strained neck (muscle involvement only)

4. If answer is "yes" to any of the above, please provide dates and details.

    _____

    _____

5.   Yes   No   Do you have vision in both eyes?
If no, please give details

_____

6.   Yes   No   Are you missing a paired organ, e.g., kidneys?
If yes, please give details

_____

7.   Yes   No   Do you wear glasses? Regular _____ Safety frames _____

8.   Yes   No   Do you wear contact lenses? Hard _____ Soft _____

9.   Do you wear any of the following?

Yes	No	permanent bridge
Yes	No	permanent crown or jacket
Yes	No	removable partial
Yes	No	full plate
Yes	No	braces

10.   Indicate if you have had any of the following during the past five (5) years:

Yes	No	fracture
Yes	No	shoulder or throwing arm injury
Yes	No	elbow injury
Yes	No	wrist injury
Yes	No	back injury
Yes	No	knee injury
Yes	No	Osgood-Schlatter's disease
Yes	No	ankle injury
Yes	No	shin splints
Yes	No	menstrual difficulties
Yes	No	surgery

11.   If the answer is "yes" to any of the above, please provide dates and details

_____

_____

12.   Yes   No   Do you have a pin, screw, or plate in your body as a result of a bone or joint surgery? If so, explain

_____

13.   Yes   No   Do you take any prescribed medications or drugs? If so, explain

_____

14.   Do you have allergies to any of the following:

Yes	No	Penicillin
Yes	No	Sulfa drugs
Yes	No	Tetracycline
Yes	No	Codeine
Yes	No	Aspirin
Yes	No	Darvon
Yes	No	bee stings
Yes	No	Tincture of Benzoin
Yes	No	other _____

15. Yes   No   Do you carrry insurance that covers you as an athlete?

Company _____

Address _____

Policy # _____

All of the above questions have been answered completely and truthfully to the best of my knowledge.

Athlete's Signature _____

Parent's/Guardian's Signature _____

Date: _____

Date _____ **Name** _____

Sport _____ **ID #** _____

1. Yes   No   Have you incurred any injury or illness since your last physical that kept you from participating in any sports or recreational activities this summer?

   If yes, please explain the circumstances below:

   Date of injury _____

   Type of injury _____

   Body part affected _____

   How did injury occur? _____

   Was a physician consulted?   Yes   No

   Additional information _____

   _____

   _____

   Date of illness _____

   Type of illness _____

   Was a physician consulted?   Yes   No

   Additional information _____

   _____

   _____

2. Yes   No   Do you have any existing problem(s) that you would like to see a physician about?

   If yes, what is the problem(s) _____

   _____

   _____

   _____

Emergency Information Card†††

Please Print

Name_____ **Birthdate**_____ **Age**_____

Parent's (Guardian) Name_____ **Home Telephone**_____

Address _____ **Grade**_____

Phone No. of Parent during Day: Father _____ **Mother**_____

In an Emergency, if Parents Cannot Be Contacted:

Notify _____ **at**_____
        (Name)   (Telephone Number)

Family Doctor _____ **Doctor's Phone** _____

Preferred Hospital_____ **Known Allergies** _____

The team physician, trainer, and coach may apply first aid treatment until the family doctor can be contacted. Yes _____ No _____

We give our consent for coaches, trainers, and team physician to use their own judgment in securing medical aid and ambulance service in case the parents cannot be reached. Yes_____ No _____

_____   _____
Date   Parent's Signature

_____

†††Reprinted with the permission of Cramer Products, Inc.

Injury Report

Name_____ **Date of Injury** _____
     last   first

Address_____ **Time of Injury**_____

Phone _____ **Location** _____

ID # _____ **Sport**_____

Classification: PE   IM   ATH   REC

Body Part Affected: (check)

Head	_____	Arm	_____	Thigh	_____
Neck	_____	Elbow	_____	Knee	_____
Shoulder	_____	Wrist	_____	Lower Leg	_____
Back	_____	Hand	_____	Ankle	_____
Chest	_____	Finger	_____	Foot	_____
Hip	_____	Other	_____		

Nature of Injury: (check)

Severe Cut	_____	Fracture	_____
Bruise	_____	Dislocation	_____
Strain	_____	Reinjury	_____
Sprain		Other	_____

Describe How Injury Occurred: **Signs and Symptoms:**

_____   _____

_____   _____

Disposition: **First Aid Rendered:**

Released _____

Student Health_____   **Supplies (Checked Out (Number):**

Family Physician_____   Elastic Bandages_____

Hospital_____   Crutches _____

_____   Other_____

Name of individual making report

_____   Returned _____ Date _____

Signature   Date

Witnesses:

(1) _____   (2) _____

Name

(1) _____   (2) _____

Address

(1) _____   (2) _____

Phone

Diagnosis: **Recommendations:**

Disposition: **Restrictions:**

No practice until (date) _____ **Prescription:**
Expected return to competition (date) _____
Return appointment (date) _____

_____
Signature   Date

Date _____

Dear Parent:

_____ has received a _____
injury of the _____. Although there is no
evidence of serious injury at this time, it would be best to follow the instructions given on the
attached sheet. Please call me at _____ or contact your family physician if you
have any questions.

_____
Coach/Trainer

_____

†††Reprinted with the permission of Cramer Products,
Inc.

Over-the-Counter Non-Rx Drugs 11

Holly Wilson, A.T.C., Ph.D.

In athletics performance is often affected by the individual's well-being. For example, at one time or another during the season, an athlete may be afflicted with a cold. The nasal congestion that usually accompanies it may profoundly affect the athlete's ability to sustain activity because oxygen exchange is restricted. Anxiety, travel, or new food experiences may alter gastrointestinal function such that the athletes develop a case of diarrhea or constipation. When attempting to deal with such problems, it is helpful if the coach has a basic understanding of the pros and cons of self-medication as well as the effectiveness of the various classes of medication available over the counter to the consumer.

Over the past few years self-medication has been advocated by the medical profession but only if the consumer is informed. For only the informed consumer can make wise decisions concerning health care. The consumer must realize that over-the-counter drugs are potentially harmful. In fact, any drug, whether it be available over the counter or only by prescription is a potential poison if improperly used. Many problems can be avoided if the medication is taken according to instructions—the recommended dosage at the proper time intervals. However, even by taking such precautions the unexpected may occur. Adverse drug reactions are not uncommon even when over-the-counter drugs are administered. Children, the elderly, and individuals under physical, mental, and emotional stress are more sensitive to drugs. For example, athletes absorb, distribute, and break down drugs faster as a result of their high metabolic rate during activity.

Important factors to keep in mind when being self-medicated are:

- use the simplest formulation available;
- check the list of ingredients before purchasing the product;
- read the instructions thoroughly *before* taking the medication;
- follow all instructions;
- consult a physician if the condition lingers on.

Presented in the next few pages is a concise summary of recommendations concerning the use of these classes of over-the-counter drugs—internal analgesic, anti-infectives, and cold remedies. For additional information, the reader is urged to consult one of the many books now available on over-the-counter medication, e.g., *The Medicine Show* published by Consumers Union.

Internal Analgesics

Internal analgesics are pain relievers and aspirin is perhaps the best known representative of this widely-used class of over-the-counter drugs. Aspirin is a valuable drug for its many and varied therapeutic effects. Besides relieving pain, the drug also reduces fever and acts as an anti-inflammatory agent.

Although the drug is available in a number of different formulations, e.g., plain, buffered, time-released, effervescent, etc., all aspirin is the same. Other than brand name, the only difference between standard five-grain tablets is price. Therefore, purchase a good quality house brand of aspirin rather than a nationally-advertised brand. However, check tablet compactness by looking at the bottom of the bottle before purchasing the brand. If the tablets are crumbling they are not compact enough and will dissolve in the mouth. On the other hand, tablets may be too compact and pass through the gastrointestinal tract without dissolving.

The most common side effect associated with regular intake of aspirin is gastrointestinal upset. Taking aspirin with a full 8-ounce glass of fluid and/or meals may alleviate the problem. If not, a buffered aspirin may reduce the discomfort enough so that diluting the aspirin with fluid is effective. As a last resort enteric-coated aspirin, which is more expensive, may be tried. The protective coating prevents the drug from dissolving until it reaches the small intestine where it is absorbed with little, if any, discomfort.

The most effective dose for pain relief is 650 mg or two five-grain aspirin tablets. Taking more tablets does not increase the onset or duration of pain relief.

A high dose of aspirin (8–16 tablets per day) is often prescribed following a musculoskeletal injury to control the inflammatory process and thus promote healing. Regardless of whether or not the condition is painful, the individual should take the aspirin as scheduled. A constant level of the analgesic must be present in the blood to cut down on the inflammation. Ringing in the ears or vertigo are two early signs of aspirin overdose. These symptoms are reversible by simply decreasing the intake of aspirin and continuing to take it on schedule.

When aspirin is prescribed on a regular basis, all medication, both prescription and over-the-counter, must be reported to the physician. Aspirin interacts with a wide variety of drugs including some as common as Vitamin C.

If the tablets begin to smell like vinegar they are decomposing and should be disposed. The effectiveness of the drug is only slightly changed but gastrointestinal irritation increases markedly.

Individuals who are allergic to aspirin may take one of the non-aspirin substitutes for pain relief or reduction of fever. Unfortunately none of the substitutes is an anti-inflammatory agent. Therefore the use of such substitutes in sports medicine is especially limited when the athlete is taking the analgesic for its anti-inflammatory effect.

Acetaminophen is the most common and most effective aspirin substitute. It does not irritate the stomach so it should be used in place of aspirin for pain relief and/or fever reduction. Phenacetin has been withdrawn from the market because its use has been associated with the development of kidney problems.

Anti-infectives

Anti-infectives are those drugs used to control the spread of infection in local tissue. Included in this class of medications are antiseptics, antifungals, and antibiotics. Whenever the skin is abraded (open) it can no longer serve as a protective barrier against foreign matter such as dirt, bacteria, fungi, etc. Even a drug may be considered foreign matter and the application of any drug to the open skin may delay healing and/or cause a medication dermatitis.

Read the instructions before applying any drug to the skin, particularly if the skin is abraded. Follow the instructions carefully and discontinue using the drug if any one of the following symptoms develop: itching; burning; blistering or redness of the skin; rash; oozing crusting dermatitis.

Antiseptics

Antiseptics are drugs applied to living tissue to kill or prevent the growth of microorganisms. However, in most instances, the body's own natural defense mechanisms can control and destroy the invading organisms.

The correct method of applying antiseptics is around the edge of the wound. Rarely should the drug be applied directly to the abraded skin. Only surface wounds should be treated at home. Treatment of deep wounds should be limited to basic first aid techniques to control bleeding and prevent further contamination and trauma. Evaluation of the extent of damage is easier for the physician when the wound remains uncleaned and untreated.

Antiseptics are classified by their major active ingredient. Only those commonly used in home treatment of surface wounds, will be discussed.

Two oxidizing agents are among the most useful antiseptics for home treatment. Three percent hydrogen peroxide is a poor antiseptic but it is useful for cleaning out contaminated surface wounds. It foams when it comes in contact with abraded skin; however, it should be applied only *after* a thorough cleansing of the wound. The presence of organic matter such as blood, cinders, grass, or dirt decreases its effectiveness. Hydrogen peroxide should be stored in a light-resistant amber bottle for it is very unstable and sensitive to light. It easily breaks down into its component parts. In fact, if the antiseptic does not foam when it comes in contact with abraded skin, it has dissociated. The other oxidizing agent recommended for home treatment is povidone-iodine. It is less irritating and less toxic than the iodine from which it is derived. It also does not stain like iodine. Unfortunately povidone-iodine is slightly less effective than iodine and is more expensive.

Perhaps the most common antiseptics found in first aid kits are two mercureal compounds—mercurochrome and merthiolate. Merthiolate is the stronger of the two. Unfortunately with the popularity of these two drugs neither one is as effective as iodine. Furthermore, the effectiveness of these two drugs is lessened by the presence of serum and tissue proteins which collect at the site of tissue damage.

Surface active agents, such as benzalkonium chloride, are frequently used as antiseptics because they do not irritate the skin. However, the antiseptics in this group may be deactivated during application by cotton, soap residue, or cellulose.

Boric acid is found in many over-the-counter products ranging from antiseptics to mouthwashes and eyewashes. It is a poor antiseptic, but more importantly, it is potentially dangerous. In some instances, it has been found to be a systemic poison.

The antiseptic that is most effective in combating microorganisms and recommended by pharmacists is Isopropyl alcohol. (Povidone-iodine is the antiseptic recommended for home- or self-treatment.) When correctly used it is the least irritating and most effective of all antiseptics. Obviously Isopropyl alcohol should not be placed directly on abraded skin but only around the edges of the wound to control the growth of microorganisms.

Antifungals

Antifungals control the growth and spread of fungal infections. Unfortunately many of the agents used as antifungals may actually aggravate an existing condition. For example, as previously mentioned, Boric acid may cause systemic toxicity in some individuals and the agent is frequently found in some products for athlete's foot, a common fungal condition. In some cases, the antifungal agent may only be strong enough to eradicate mild cases. Undecylenic acid, an ingredient in many over-the-counter products for athlete's foot, will control a mild case but not clear it up. Tolnaftate is the most effective antifungal agent for self-medication, yet the consumer must pay the price for such effectiveness. Products containing tolnaftate are more expensive than those containing other antifungal agents.

Unfortunately to irradicate a case of athlete's foot completely, the agent must be applied for up to six months, even though evidence of the disease is not visible. New growths from the spores that remain in the area must be controlled.

Antibiotics

Antibiotics are topically applied to inhibit the growth and reproduction of bacteria. Most are highly specific meaning they are effective at controlling only certain bacteria. Such agents should be used sparingly for a strain of bacteria can easily become resistant with overuse of the ointment. In addition, allergic reactions are not common.

The antibiotics commonly found in over-the-counter ointments are neomycin, bacitracin, and polymyxin B sulfate. The three may be found in combination or separately. Most often the body defenses can effectively control the growth of any bacteria remaining in or around the wound following a thorough cleansing. However, if signs of infection (heat, redness, swelling, pain, and point tenderness) develop, the individual should be immediately referred to a physician.

Cold Remedies

The common cold is a self-limiting disease which lasts for one to two weeks and is caused by a virus. Since there are a multitude of viruses that could be responsible for the upper respiratory tract infection characteristic of a cold, medical science has yet to isolate a cure. At this time, the best the consumer can hope for is symptomatic relief.

In attempting to alleviate symptoms, the consumer has two choices in self-treatment: to use a variety of single ingredient products; to use one combination product, frequently referred to as a shotgun remedy. The rationale behind shotgun remedies is if a medication is to be effective at relieving the multitude of symptoms associated with the common cold, it must contain a little bit of everything. In reality, however, there are a few drawbacks to such thinking. First, all the various ingredients found in a shotgun remedy may not be needed if the individual is not suffering from all the symptoms the remedy is designed to relieve. Secondly, there may not be enough of any one ingredient to be therapeutically effective. Thirdly, there is a greater chance of an adverse reaction occurring as the medication becomes more complex. In most instances, it is far wiser, therapeutically and economically, for the individual to purchase single-ingredient medications and only take those necessary to relieve the symptoms being displayed.

Antihistamines and Decongestants

Nasal congestions is perhaps the chief complaint of one who suffers from a cold. In seeking relief, the consumer must make a decision whether to use an antihistamine or a decongestant. With a little basic background information, the choice may not be so difficult to make.

The effects of antihistamines are essentially the same. An antihistamine, as the name applies, blocks the release of histamine. Histamine, as well as several other chemical mediators, are released by cells following invasion of the body by a virus. It is these chemical mediators that are responsible for the dilation of capillaries in the mucus membrane lining the respiratory tract and the resulting congestion. Therefore, an antihistamine is not totally effective at relieving a stuffy nose for its target is only one of the many chemical mediators. The common side-effects associated with the use of an antihistamine are drowsiness, dry mouth, and blurred vision. Obviously in athletics the use of such medication should be restricted for the athlete should be mentally and physically alert when in play. Furthermore, the use of antihistamines by an athlete who is active in a hot, humid environment may predispose that individual to one of the heat stress syndromes. Constriction of the superficial blood vessels interferes with effective cooling of the body.

The congested athlete can find relief from the use of decongestants but these products, too, are not without problems. The drug may be administered, either topically, as a nasal spray, or orally. If used too frequently a nasal spray may actually cause nasal congestion. The drug shrinks the mucus membrane so effectively that it interferes with the lining's protective function. Consequently more mucus is secreted so the lining can once again trap foreign material on its sticky surface. This rebound effect occurs each time the spray is used so the consumer is just perpetrating the condition. A nasal spray should be used as directed for no more than 2-3 times a day for 3-4 days. Use of a long-duration spray decreases the possibility of rebound congestion.

Oral administration of a decongestant poses less of a problem. The major side-effects are nervousness and restlessness as well as excessive dryness of the nose, mouth, and throat. Relief is not as great with oral administration because the drug is carried in the blood stream to all the various mucus membranes in the body. The action is more generalized than with a nasal spray.

Cough Remedies

A cough is a protective reflex, therefore it should not be eliminated completely, even though the cough may not be productive and is merely self-perpetuating. A cough medicine or antitussive only controls the frequency and severity of a cough but does not alleviate it.

There are three types of cough medicine available to the consumer: central acting agents; expectorants; demulcents. Common central acting agents are dextromethorphan and codeine, the latter being a prescription drug. Both are effective in reducing the frequency and intensity of a cough, but dextromethorphan is recommended for self-treatment. It has none of the side-effects associated with the use of the narcotic codeine. Expectorants such as ammonium chloride or terpin hydrate increase fluid production and help mobilize secretions. Demulcents coat the irritated tissue and stimulate saliva production. Wild cherry, honey, and licorice are common demulcents that are frequently found in cough drops. Such preparations, however, are no more effective than plain hard candy in soothing irritated tissue.

Prior to purchasing a cough medicine, pay particular attention to the percent of alcohol in the product. Although alcohol is a depressant of the central nervous system, it also dries up the mucus membrane and would thus cause additional irritation.

In self-treatment the consumer should attempt to mobilize secretions and sooth the irritated tissue by sucking on plain hard candy, drinking hot beverages, and inhaling steam. In the latter instance, if a vaporizer is not readily available, an effective substitute can easily be made. Bring a pan of water to a boil and then turn off the heating source. Place a towel over the individual's head to form a tent and thus confine vapors. Instruct the individual to breathe deeply.

Sore Throat Remedies

Among the common complaints of the cold sufferer is a sore throat; however, this condition may be of bacterial origin rather than viral. It is important to identify the cause particularly if the sore throat lingers on for more than 2 days and/or is accompanied by a fever. Sore throats caused by either streptococcus or staphylococcus bacteria are far more dangerous because complications involving the heart or kidneys could arise as a result of improper or delayed treatment. Fortunately, bacterial infections are not as common as viral infections and in most instances, antibiotics are effective in treating them. (Antibiotics are not effective against viral infections). If a 10-day course of antibiotics is prescribed by a physician the entire amount must be taken to control the disease process. Do not stop taking the medication just because symptoms improve or disappear.

Other than aspirin there are few over-the-counter products that are helpful in relieving the symptoms of a sore throat. To be effective the aspirin must be taken orally and absorbed into the blood stream. If used in a gargle, the inflamed tissue could be easily irritated by one of the acid particles in the water. Antiseptic gargles and mouthwashes may contain alcohol which is an irritant as previously explained. Throat lozengers, especially those with an antibacterial agent or an anaesthetic agent are frequently associated with sensitivity reactions.

In treating a sore throat the consumer should avoid all over-the-counter preparations other than aspirin and gargle with warm salt water. The mixture is made by adding ½ teaspoon of salt to 8 ounces or one cup of warm water. If the condition persists for more than two days or is accompanied by a fever, medical attention should be sought.

Miconceptions of Athletic Injuries 12

Linda Arnold, A.T.C.

Education of athletic trainers, coaches, and athletes is necessary to eliminate the misconceptions involving athletic injuries. These misconceptions have arisen from certain "traditions" among athletes and coaches who have previously been misinformed as to the proper way to evaluate and treat injuries. No longer should athletes be subjected to the "walk it off" attitude of coaches. The level of competitiveness has advanced tremendously, and the rate of injuries has also increased. Without a proper evaluation or a knowledge of significant warning symptoms, a very serious symptom may be overlooked which could be detrimental to the athlete's future.

It should be noted that if a physician's care is needed, it is vital for the athlete to be seen by someone with a background and/or interest in sports medicine. For possible bone and muscle injuries, an orthopedic physician should be seen; for possible nerve damage a neurologist should be seen, and so forth. Many general practitioners, or family doctors, may very well have an inadequate background in specific medical problems, such as orthopedic problems, which compromise the majority of athletic injuries.

Prevention of injury is important in all aspects of athletics. There are many injuries which cannot be prevented. However, the incidence of muscle strains can be reduced with proper stretching exercises. Athletes are told to "warm-up" before participation. This might be interpreted as a means for warming up the skin with the use of an analgesic balm. These products are skin irritants and produce a warm sensation on the surface of the skin. Once the skin is warm, the athlete thinks he/she is "warmed up" and ready to play. He/she has unintentionally been misled and therefore does not understand the meaning or purpose of "warm-

ing up" with proper stretching techniques which could prevent a muscle strain.

Without the care of a certified athletic trainer to provide evaluation of injuries when they occur, the athletes may be put in danger. The coach should have a good background in recognizing serious symptoms and *must* know proper first aid procedures.

For the majority of athletic injuries, the basic treatment consists of ice, compression, and elevation. Placing heat on a new injury or placing the injured area in a hot whirlpool will only cause serious complications. Heat causes an increase in blood flow which, in turn, causes unnecessary swelling in damaged tissues. Heat may very well be used later for rehabilitative purposes, but can only complicate the treatment if used when the injury initially occurs.

There are several misconceptions in recognizing symptoms of injuries. It is assumed by many that if an injured area can be moved, it is not fractured. "Broken" and "fractured" are both terms used to describe a crack or break in a bone. The seriousness of a fracture may range from a small crack (hairline fracture) in the bone to a complete break. Most fractured areas *can* be moved; the athlete may not desire to move it, but movement may be possible. Therefore, other symptoms of a fracture are much more important to consider in this injury evaluation.

Swelling is another important symptom. If swelling does occur, it is assumed that there has been significant tissue damage. However, swelling cannot be an all-inclusive evaluative tool. An athlete may sustain a major ligament or tendon tear and develop little swelling, or, the athlete may merely rupture a superficial blood vessel which results in rapid swelling but is actually an insignificant injury. The amount of swelling cannot be used to measure the seriousness of an injury. Proper evaluation of the injury is necessary to determine its seriousness.

As with swelling, pain also cannot be a conclusive determining factor in injury evaluations. Athletes differ in levels of pain tolerance as much as they differ in levels of skill. An athlete with a major injury may experience minimal pain. On the other hand, an athlete with a low pain tolerance may experience tremendous pain with a minor injury. Also, it is often difficult for an athlete who has never been injured to distinguish the difference between pain and injury. Pain can often be a warning signal, but does not always signify damage to a body part.

There is another thing to consider with regard to pain after an injury. During an injury which results in a complete rupture of a ligament, the pain may be intense during the injury and then subside somewhat following the severance of the ligament. If the pain subsides and if there happens to be little swelling following the injury, the athlete may delay seeing a physician and jeopardize his/her chance for an adequate recovery.

It is often felt that the athlete has the right to play with an injury if he/she so consents. However, proper evaluation procedures must take place so that all possible complications can be considered before allowing the athlete to make this decision. Most schools accept the responsibility of seeking a physician's care for athletic injuries. Should there be any chance of further injury by participating with an injury, it would be *very* inadvisable to leave the decision up to the athlete if the attending physician prescribed no participation. So, in fact, the final decision rests with the athlete with respect to *not* playing, but should be the physician's decision with regard to playing *with* an injury.

The appearance of braces and protective taping is much more prevalent now in women's athletics. It should be strongly advised that neither taping nor braces be used without a specific reason. The theory of "if it hurts, tape it up" has got to be eliminated from athletics. Taping should only be used to restrict a specific movement or to support an injured area. If tape is not properly used, the athlete can suffer from its use, rather than benefit from it. Improperly used taping techniques could result in swelling, restricted circulation, pressure on nerves, tape cuts, blisters, etc. Therefore, it becomes necessary for coaches to receive instructions on taping techniques to educate them on this common practice.

Although taping is fairly common, the use of braces has become almost as popular. In no way should a brace be placed on an athlete without a physician's consent. Braces are often placed on athletes for psychological support. However, the use of psychological "tricks" should be avoided if at all possible. Good, sound rehabilitation programs can often restore an injured athlete back to a near normal condition which may not require the use of a brace.

Recently, a concern in women's athletics has been the use of protective equipment to further avoid injuries to the "frail" female athlete. It is often necessary to use protective equipment for specific needs of certain athletes. However, to use all the protective equipment available would result in an athlete being dressed in eye goggles, a mouthguard, a neck collar, a sports bra, hip pads, knee pads, elbow pads, knee braces, ankle braces, etc. Common sense must be used to find the best method to prevent injury in each specific sport. Protective equipment may, in fact, be a means of prevention, but one should not go overboard in this area.

A commonly mistreated injury among athletes is that of a "jammed" finger. The traditional treatment has been to immediately pull the finger. This treatment should be strongly avoided. A "jammed" finger usually consists of sprained ligaments surrounding a joint in the finger. This sprain may involve a simple stretching or a complete rupture of the ligaments. If the ligaments are partially torn, they may be completely ruptured by pulling on the finger. An injured finger may be the result of a fracture in the joint area. It is not possible to eliminate the possibility of a fracture without first examining an x-ray of the injury. Therefore, it should be assumed that a fracture may be present. Another possibility involving fractures of this area is the fact that a piece of bone may be chipped off. Manipulation of the finger may allow this fragment of bone to lodge in the joint. Surgery would then be required to dislodge the bone fragment, causing this somewhat minor injury to develop into a major problem.

The American Medical Association has developed a Bill of Rights for athletes. Under this Bill, athletes have the right to good health supervision. With regard to the previously-mentioned misconceptions, this right has been violated in many ways. Adequate care of athletes, provided by educating coaches or securing the services of a certified athletic trainer, is the most accurate way to eliminate these traditional ill-advised practices. Athletes have suffered long enough from the results of these misconceptions. Every effort should be made by athletic organizations to provide the best possible care for their athletes.

"Get the Gum out"

Perhaps the most dangerous misconception among athletes is the concept that chewing gum will not hinder their performance. There has always been concern for the best techniques for preventing injuries. However, the very act of chewing gum while participating in athletics may cause a very potential life and death situation. It is very frustrating to see a coach or even an athletic trainer pass out gum to a team before a game. These same people are often the ones who are most concerned about preventing all types of injuries, but do not make the effort to prevent a possible death.

Comments such as "I've chewed gum all my life while playing and I've never gotten choked" do not prevent this type of death. Those athletes who have died from this condition probably felt the same way. This accident does not happen often but it only takes one time, and a few minutes at that, to kill an athlete. Coaches who allow gum chewing may have never realized the possible serious consequences which could follow. Education of athletes and coaches is essential to eliminating this traditional practice.

Those who feel the risk is slim and continue to allow gum chewing should at least make the effort to learn the proper techniques of clearing an obstructed airway.

The problem with chewing gum develops if the athlete gets hit unexpectedly from the rear, or if he/she gets knocked unconscious. A review of the anatomy of the throat shows the location of the airway, or trachea. The trachea (A) lies under the skin on the front of the neck. The passage for food, the esophagus (B) lies behind the trachea. When swallowing occurs the epiglottis (C) covers the opening of the trachea and prevents food from entering the airway.

An unexpected blow from the rear can very easily cause the head to be thrown back, straighten the airway, and permit the gum to lodge in the airway (D). To dislodge the gum from this area, proper techniques in administering the Heimlich Maneuver would be necessary.

The American Red Cross currently teaches three maneuvers for the removal of airway obstructions: back blow; abdominal thrust (Heimlich Maneuver); probing the mouth. It takes a very short time to learn, but the results of its use may mean the difference between life or death. It should be emphasized that a person receive proper training in this technique to fully understand the procedure. It must also be noted that this procedure should never be practiced on another person due to possible internal injuries.

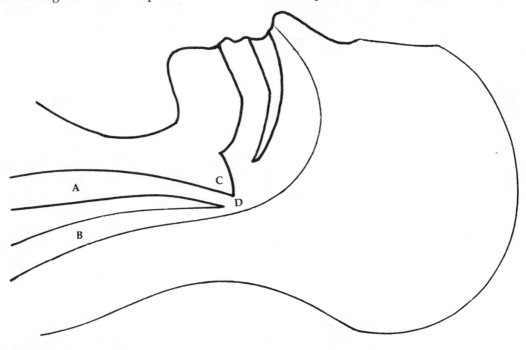

Figure 1. Anatomy of the throat.

Jewelry Hazards

Uncommon among men athletes, but very common among women athletes, is the wearing of jewelry during participation. If jewelry is attractive when not playing, why would it not be attractive *while* playing? Individual team sport participants can most likely wear jewelry and have few problems. It is very common to see tennis players and golfers wearing several pieces of jewelry. However, for those athletes in contact sports (or any sport for that matter), this practice should be avoided. Injuries to the athlete and the opponent could very likely occur.

Rings can cause serious problems when the athlete sustains a finger injury. If swelling is immediate, the ring most likely would have to be cut from the finger. Rings can also cause injuries by scraping or hitting an opponent. Should a ring get caught on some piece of equipment, the results could be a dislocated or amputated finger.

Necklaces are a cause of many serious eye injuries. This most often happens to an opponent as a long necklace hits the individual in the eye. Should the necklace get caught on equipment, an opponent's clothing, or on the athlete's hand, etc., an unnecessary injury could occur.

One of the most popular trends in jewelry now is the use of beads in braided hair styles. Although these are felt to be attractive by many, they are definite hazards in athletics. Like necklaces the longer sets of beads are flying objects in an opponent's face and should not be permitted in contact sports.

By not permitting the wearing of jewelry, a coach may prevent some very unnecessary injuries. Athletes have to contend with the threat of many injuries which cannot be prevented. Therefore every effort should be made to eliminate those which can be prevented.

The Female Athlete

Christine Haycock, M.D., F.A.C.S.

13

During the past decade there has been much controversy as to just how important the anatomical and physiological differences are between male and female athletes. In general the average female is shorter and lighter than the average male. There are exceptions to this of course, but the bone structure of the female is definitely lighter than the male and there is less lean muscle mass.

A major difference between men and women is the amount of body fat. A typical young woman's body has about 25% body weight of fat while a young man would have about 15%. While athletes of both sexes are probably thinner than the average sedentary subject, nevertheless this difference persists. A female long-distance runner may drop down to as low as 7% body fat, while men can often drop as low as 5%.

Another difference is that men have their major reproductive organs externally carried in the scrotum, whereas women have the advantage of having their reproductive organs carefully protected within the bony pelvis. In this sense women are better protected for contact sports than men.

Women's breasts are more developed than males, since these organs are basically intended for the reproductive purposes of nursing infants. However, many women athletes may have very small breasts and this can be an advantage, for example, in a long-distance runner. The vulnerability of the breast to injury has been grossly overrated and, in general, injuries to the breasts are minor and of no serious consequence.

Women have a wider pelvis than men and therefore their center of gravity is lower than that of men. This can be an advantage or it can be a disadvantage. The female athlete playing tennis might be more stable in the ready position than a male, but on the other hand she would have more difficulty lifting her body off the ground for any type of jumping activity. This development of the hips becomes more obvious as the female becomes older, hence it accounts for one of the reasons why the best women gymnasts are usually in their early teens.

In the past the wider female pelvis and the resulting greater angulation of the femur on the pelvis had been attributed as the cause of increased injuries to women's knees. More recently, however, it has been shown that these injuries are more likely related to poor conditioning than anatomical development. With an increase in conditioning programs for women, less knee injuries are being recorded.

Women do tend to be more bowlegged than men and this can cause stress to the outside of the knees and ankles. A woman who is bowlegged should buy shoes that cant to the inside to increase pronation, and thus avoid knee injuries. On the other hand, should a woman be knocked-kneed she should find shoes that reduce the pronation with a wedge built into the sole to alleviate the stress to the inside of the knees, ankles, and feet.

Much has been made of the fact that women have more laxity in their joints than men. However, there are also many men who have "loose" joints which does not pose as a great problem providing that a good conditioning program is carried out to strengthen the joints. It is an advantage for the gymnast and the dancer, and with a good conditioning program does not lead to any more sprained ankles or other difficulties than the average male athlete may encounter.

Back problems in women are more prominent due to the fact that their spines have a greater curvature (lordosis). There is also a congenital condition called spondylolisthesis in which there is a slippage of the lower vertebrae of the spine which, if not recognized early in the teen years, can lead to many problems later in the female athlete, particularly for the gymnast. Hence, with a good conditioning program and the avoidance of such sports as gymnastics this individual can perform normally in sports not requiring marked flexion of the back. Because women do tend to have more back problems, and also tend to be a little pot-bellied, it is extremely important that exercises that strengthen the abdominal musculature as well as the back muscles be carried out, and that attention be paid to posture. Women must learn to tuck in their tummies and straighten their backs to avoid problems. lems.

Because there is less muscular development in women, due to less male hormones (testosterone), women do not have the upper extremity and shoulder strength that most men do. This accounts for their difficulty in doing pull-ups. Pitching motions in softball, particular in the fast pitch variety, can cause more problems in women than men for this reason, and can result in overuse problems such as tendonitis. More recently the lifting of weights and the use of various types of gymnastic apparatus to increase the upper body strength in women have proved to be most valuable in the prevention of difficulties in the shoulders and arms and has increased performances in women athletes.

It has been suggested that women should be encouraged to enter a sport that was most suitable for their own body type. A tall skinny woman will do well in track and field and fast-moving sports, whereas the heavier, squattier type of female would probably do better in softball, disc, and javelin throwing, and other sports in which her low center of gravity can be to an advantage.

It might be wise for the coach or trainer to take a careful look at his/her female athletes to determine their body types and to anticipate problems that might arise from marked lordosis, wide heavy hips, or the lack of upper body development and place them into training programs to correct any deficiencies and also pay close attention to the type of shoes, for example, that are worn by these women.

Other differences in women are less obvious since they are hormonal in nature and have to do with the fact that a woman menstruates. Women athletes who have heavy menstrual cycles may tend to be a little anemic so it is important that these women use supplemental iron during their menstrual period to avoid an iron deficiency anemia that could interfere with oxygen uptake in endurance sports. A simple blood test can determine this and a quick resolution of the problem can be made.

There has been much discussion recently over the amenorrhea seen in women athletes and considerable discussion has ensued as to whether or not this is a problem that should concern the athlete or not. So far the evidence has not shown any really deleterious effects if the athlete who lessens strenuous training resumes her period in a short time. If the female athlete does not resume normal periods following cessation of heavy training, then it is advisable that she see a gynecologist and ensure a good hormonal balance so that no future problems will occur. There certainly is no decrease in fertility in women athletes who have undergone rigorous training. Positive evidence indicates that girls who exercise have less problems with dysmenorrhea.

Some recent studies have suggested that women on birth control pills may lack certain nutrient substances in their bodies and research is continuing along these lines; however, it is generally felt that the athlete who eats a well-balanced diet with perhaps a mineral and vitamin supplement, particularly during her menstrual period, is in no great danger of this.

A woman who is large-breasted will probably need a good supportive bra to limit the motion of the breasts relative to the rest of her body since large pendulous breasts can definitely throw an athlete off stride, or prove to be a detriment to good competitive effort. There are many bras now on the market made of a high cotton and low polyester mixture which will provide support and comfort to obviate the problem.

Another condition that women are more prone to is thyroid disorders. Should there be any problems associated with persistent weight gain or rapid weight loss, change in hair body distribution, excessive sweating, etc., it would be wise to have some blood tests done to determine if there is any hyper- or hypothyroidism present which needs to be corrected.

Women tend to bruise more easily than men because they have greater capillary fragility. A woman athlete who tends to bruise more readily than her teammates can be placed on supplemental Vitamin C to reduce as much as possible the tendency to rupture her capillaries with minor blows. Except for the fact that bruises are nasty looking, they really pose no serious problems.

Pregnancy poses no great restrictions on athletic endeavors in the first trimester if the women are having an uneventful pregnancy. However, beyond the first trimester, it is considered inadvisable for her to endulge in contact sports. Any other restrictions necessary would have to be determined by her physician and the progress of the pregnancy.

Research has indicated that the injuries seen in female athletes are really no different than those seen in the male except for those few directly related to anatomical differences. Therefore, with good conditioning programs and proper nutrition, the woman athlete should have no more difficulties endulging in sports than her male counterpart.

The Growing Athlete

Holly Wilson, A.T.C.

The growing athlete is prone to different sorts of sport injuries than the mature athlete because the individual's musculoskeletal system is immature. During childhood and adolescence, the skeleton is in a constant process of ossification in which cartilage is converted to rigid bone. At the end of each long bone are growth centers where longitudinal growth takes place. It is this ossification process that accounts for such growth. The greatest activity in these growth centers, and hence the most rapid gains in height and limb length, is seen during childhood between the ages of 5½ and 7 and during adolescence between the ages of 9 and 12 in females and 13 and 15 in males. It is not until approximately the mid-teens in females and the late teens to the early twenties in males that the last of these growth centers close and skeletal maturity is attained. Until maturity occurs, these growth centers are the weakest part of the musculoskeletal system.

A typical long bone has several growth centers. (See Figure 1.) The end of the bone including its smooth articular cartilage lining is the epiphysis. It is a secondary ossification center. Separating the epiphysis from the shaft of the long bone is the growth plate or physis. The physis is the primary ossification center for the bone. It is made up of cartilage and it is the area where growth in length occurs. Where a muscle attaches to a bony prominence, each prominence has a separate growth center called an apophysis. The shaft of the bone is called the diaphysis and the tough membrane covering the entire long bone except the smooth articular cartilage ends is the periosteum. The periosteum protects the underlying bone and houses the blood vessels that bring nourishment.

There are four types of injuries seen in the growing athlete that may not be seen in the mature athlete. Three of these injuries in-

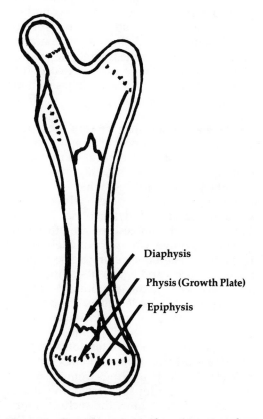

Figure 1. Growth centers of an immature long bone.

Diaphysis

Physis (Growth Plate)

Epiphysis

volve the various growth centers: the epiphysis; the physis; the apophysis. Consequently, they are only seen in the growing athlete.

The epiphysis may be traumatized by a compression force such as landing from a fall or a jump. With impact between the bone ends, small pieces may partially or completely separate from the epiphysis. As a result of complete separation, the chips of bone with cartilage float freely within the joint space and are called "joint mice." If these chips become symptomatic (cause pain, swelling, etc.) and interfere with the function of the joint, they may need to be surgically removed. Those that remain partially attached may eventually reattach and pose little, if any, problem. The ankle and the knee are common sites for "joint mice."

The physis or growth plate is susceptible to damage from a direct blow or a twisting motion. Either force may shear through the growth plate and dislocate the epiphysis from the underlying shaft of the bone, the diaphysis. The injury is called an epiphyseal separation and may result in growth complications; however, the incidence of such problems is low. There are several factors that contribute to the development of a complication: the age of the athlete; the specific growth plate involved; the type of separation (one of four grades); the immediate medical attention given. Grade one or two epiphyseal separations rarely result in loss of limb length, angular deformity, or joint malfunction.

A muscle tendon may be torn loose (avulsed) from its attachment at an apophysis as a result of pivoting, running, jumping, or twisting. At an apophysis, the muscle tendon attaches to cartilage which is not as strong as an attachment directly into the periosteum and underlying bone. Furthermore, during the adolescent growth spurt, flexibility is outgrown approximately every six months. The bones elongate so rapidly that the muscles and ligaments cannot keep up. Consequently, the individual is inflexible and prone to muscle injury. The damage, however, may be an avulsion of an apophysis rather than to the muscle, musculotendinous junction, or tendon as seen in the mature athlete. Common sites for such avulsions are the hamstrings from the ischial tuberosity, the iliopsoas from the lesser trochanter of the femur, the rectus femoris from the anterior inferior iliac spine, and the abdominals from the iliac crest. The incidence of such injuries can be decreased by working on a daily statis stretching program and thoroughly warming up prior to each activity session.

The fourth type of injury is the stress fracture which one sees more frequently in the 6-21 age group than in the mature athlete. As the name implies, stress fractures are the result of repetitive stress causing an eventual breakdown of bony structure and hence, an incomplete fracture. If the athlete continues the repetitive activity, the stress fracture may become a complete fracture. Another fracture that may also be seen in this age group is a pathological fracture. Such a fracture occurs where there is a defect in the growing bone. The force causing the injury is usually insignificant but the weakened structure is unable to withstand the stress.

In the growing athlete, the musculoskeletal system appears to be vulnerable. Yet there are certain anatomical and physiological characteristics of the youthful system that provide some compensation for and protection against trauma. The bones of the growing athlete are porous, that is, they bend with the force, absorbing and dissipating the impact rather than resisting it like the strong rigid bones of the mature athlete. Such a bone can bend to a 45° angle or more before breaking. If the bone does break, the break is usually incomplete, a greenstick fracture. If it does not break, the bone will straighten out but not completely. Medical care should be sought, for this injury is also considered to be a type of fracture called a bend fracture. The periosteum, the membrane covering the bone, is thicker and stronger in growing athletes. It has greater potential for repair and replacement of damaged cells because it has more bone-forming cells. In addition, it has a better blood supply to accomodate healing as well as growth. Consequently, healing is more rapid, but the time required for mending increases with each year of age. Nonunion of fractures is almost unheard of in this age group. Fractures in growing athletes are more stable than in the mature athlete. The tough periosteum resists tearing and the break is often incomplete so there is less play, if any, in the broken bone ends. As a result, involvement of the adjacent blood vessels and nerves is not as common. Finally, fractures in growing athletes have a tendency to remodel. The body attempts to correct any discrepency in bony configuration resulting from a fracture. Remodelling, like the healing rate, is inversely related to age. Furthermore, the closer the injury site is to the physis or growth plate, the more likely it is that remodelling will occur.

Musculoskeletal injuries in growing athletes should be treated conservatively until the possibility of growth center involvement is ruled out. Dislocations and isolated ligament tears are uncommon in this age group because ligaments are stronger than the growth centers. With an injury to the physis or growth plate, pain and/or deformity will be immediately localized above or below the joint, not at the joint space. The growing athlete may have difficulty pinpointing the pain, for it is often referred to other parts of the body. Be sure to check all the areas identified by the athlete as being painful.

Treat all suspected epiphyseal separations as if they were fractures. Apply compression with a wet elastic bandage and splint the involved joint as well as the adjacent joints. Place an ice pack over the area and elevate the part. Keep the ice pack in place for no more than 20-30 minutes. (Ice may be applied again and repeated in 1½-2 hour intervals.) Make arrangements for the athlete to be seen by a physician.

Although the musculoskeletal system of the growing athlete is immature, the incidence of serious injury to the system, including injuries to the growth centers, is not high. The growing athlete, particularly the younger one, does not usually have the size and strength to generate enough force to cause serious injury. This is important, for during periods of rapid growth when the muscles and ligaments are outgrown, the muscles do not have the strength to protect the musculoskeletal system from trauma. Furthermore, it must be realized that there are risks involved in most of the activities in which children engage. In fact, the activity would not be considered fun unless some element of daredevilry was a part of the activity.

Appendix
Bibliography

Abraham, William M. "Exercise-induced Muscle Soreness." *The Physician and Sportsmedicine*. October, 1979, pp. 57–66.

Adolph, E. F. "Heat Injuries during Distance Running." *Medicine and Science in Sports*. July, 1975, p. 1.

Allman, F. "Prevention of Sport Injuries." *Athletic Journal*. March, 1976.

Alwine, Daryle. "What You Should Know about Osgood-Schlatter's Disease." *Athletic Journal* 56:72–3.

Anthony, Susan. "Taping Techniques." 1) The Ankle—*Athletic Journal* 57:72–3; 2) The Achilles Tendon—*Athletic Journal* 57:14–5; The Longitudinal Arch—*Athletic Journal* 57:68–9.

Barnes, Lan. "Cryotherapy—Putting Injury on Ice." *The Physician and Sportsmedicine*. June, 1979, pp. 130–6.

Bentivegna, Angelo. "Diet, Fitness and Athletic Performance." *The Physician and Sportsmedicine*. October, 1979, pp. 98–105.

Bergfield, John. "First, Second and Third Degree Sprains." *The American Journal of Sports Medicine*. May/June, 1979.

Blonstein, S. L. "Concussion." *The Journal of Sport Medicine and Physical Fitness* 17: 79–81.

Bodner, Leslie. "Historical Poll of Women in Sports." *The American Journal of Sports Medicine*. January-February, 1980, pp. 54–5.

Bonnette, Allen R. "Using the Swimming Pool to Rehabilitate Injuries." *Athletic Journal* 59.

Boyd, Harold, and McLeod, Jr., Andin. "Tennis Elbow." *Journal of Bone and Joint Surgery*. September, 1973, pp. 1183–7.

Brooks, Christine. "Developing the Female Distance Runner." *Athletic Journal*. January, 1978, pp. 8, 10, 80, and 81.

Brown, Harvey C. "Common Injuries of the Athlete's Hand." *Canadian Medical Association Journal*. September 17, 1977, pp. 621–5.

Brubaker, Clifford E. "Injuries to Runners." *Journal of Sportsmedicine*. July/August, 1974, pp. 1189–98.

Cahill, B. R. "Osgood-Schlatter Disease in Competitive Sports." *Journal of the American Medical Association*. January 9, 1978, p. 143.

Cahill, Bernard R. "Little League Shoulder." *Journal of Sports Medicine*. May-June, 1974, pp. 1515–53.

Cahill, Bernard, and Griffith, Edward. "Effect of Preseason Conditioning on the Incidence and Severity of High School Football Knee Injuries." *The American Journal of Sports Medicine*. July-August, 1979, pp. 180–4.

Clancy, W. G.; Micheli, L. J.; Jackson, D. W.; and Stanich, W. "Low Back Pain in Young and Middle-aged Athletes." *The American Journal of Sports Medicine*. July, 1979.

Clancy, William G., and Neidhart, David. "Achilles Tendonitis in Runners." *The American Journal of Sports Medicine* 4.

Cleary, Pat. "The Caloric Costs of Rope Skipping." *The Physician and Sportsmedicine*. February, 1980, pp. 23–32.

Cooper, David. "Hamstring Strains." *Physician and Sportsmedicine* 6 (Part 2).

Cooper, Donald. "Traumatic Bursitis." *Physician and Sportsmedicine* 6 (Part I).

Cooper, Donald. "Treatment of Hip Pointers." *Physician and Sportsmedicine* 6 (Part I).

Cooper, Donald, and Fair, Jeff. "Contact Dermitis." *The Physician and Sportsmedicine*. December, 1978, pp. 123–7.

Cooper, Donald L., and Fair, Jeff. "Preventing Chest and Upper Abdominal Pain Associated with Exercise." *The Physician and Sportsmedicine*. July, 1977, pp. 93–4.

Coutts, Kenneth D. "Leg Power and Canadian Female Volleyball Players." *Research Quarterly*. October, 1976, pp. 332–5.

Cox, Jay. "Injury Nomenclature." *The American Journal of Sports Medicine*. May-June, 1979, pp. 211–3.

Cox, Jay S. "Women in Sports: the Naval Academy Experience." *The American Journal of Sports Medicine*. November/December, 1979.

Crava, Sakari, and Saarela, Jussi. "Exertion Injuries to Young Athletes, a Follow-up Research on Orthopedic Problems of Young Track and Field Athletes." *The American Journal of Sports Medicine*. July-August, 1979, pp. 180–4.

Crobitt, R. W., et al. "Female Athletics." *Journal of the American Medical Association*. June 3, 1974, pp. 1266–7.

Dale, Edwin. "Reproductive Physiology of the Female Distance Runner." *The Physician and Sportsmedicine 7*: 83–95.

Darden, Ellington. "Nutrition for Athletes." *Sports Medicine Newsletter.* 1980.

Davies, George C. "The Ankle Wrap: Variation for the Traditional." *Athletic Training 12* (4): 194–7.

Day, M. J. "Hypersensitive Response to Ice Massage." *Physical Therapy 54*(6): 592.

Dehaven, Kenneth, et al. "Chondramalacia Patellae in Athletes." *American Journal of Sports Medicine 7*(1): 5–11.

Dosti, Rose. "Diet and Athletic Training Capacity." *Swimming World & Junior Swimmer 19*(6): 43–4.

Drissoff, William B. "Runner's Injuries." *The Physician and Sportsmedicine.* December, 1979, pp. 53–64.

Engerbreton, David L. "The Diabetic in Physical Education, Recreation and Athletics." *Journal of Physical Education and Recreation.* April, 1977, pp. 18–21.

Fairbanks, Leland. "Return to Sport Participation." *The Physician and Sportsmedicine.* August, 1979.

Feigel, William P. "The Runner's Knee." *Runner's World.* May, 1980, pp. 37–40.

Ferris, Elizabeth. "The Myths Surrounding Women's Participation in Sport and Exercise." *Journal of Sports Medicine 19* (3): 309–11.

Fimrite, Ron. "Stress, Strain and Pain." *Sports Illustrated.* August, 1978, pp. 30–3.

Fowler, Peter. "Shoulder Problems in Overhead-overuse Sports." *American Journal of Sports Medicine.* March/April, 1979, pp. 141–2.

Francis, R.; Bunch, T.; and Chandler, B. "Little League Elbow: a Decade Later." *The Physician and Sportsmedicine.* April, 1978.

Fultz, Jack. "Coping with Injuries." *The Runner 16.*

Garrick, J. G., and Requa, R. K. "Injury Patterns in Children and Adolescent Skiers." *The American Journal of Sports Medicine.* July/August, 1979.

Gelabert, Raoul. "Preventing Dancers' Injuries." *The Physician and Sportsmedicine.* April, 1980, pp. 69–74.

Getchell, Bud. "The Caloric Costs of Rope Skipping and Running." *The Physician and Sportsmedicine. 8* (2): 55–60.

Glover, Elbert. "Aspirin: Is It the Next Wonder Drug for Everyone." *Runner's World.* April, 1980, pp. 67–70.

Grimes, Donald W., and Bennion, David. "Functional Foot-reconditioning Exercises." *American Journal of Sports Medicine 6*(4): 194–7.

Harris, D. V. "Lazy Bones: Shake a Leg—or Break It." *Women's Sports 5*(2): 55.

Harris, Dorothy V. "The Anemic Athlete." *Women Sports.* December, 1977.

Harris, Dorothy V. "The Monthly Mystery." *Women Sports.* September, 1977.

Harris, Dorothy V. "The Pregnant Athlete." *Women Sports.* June, 1977.

Harris, Dorothy V. "Survival of the Sweatiest." *Women Sports.* November, 1977, p. 48.

Haycock, Christine. "Susceptibility of Women Athletes to Injury: Myths vs. Reality." *Journal of the American Medical Association.* July, 1976, pp. 163–5.

Hoffman, Terrence; Stouffer, Robert; and Jackson, Andrew. "Differences in Strength between the Sexes." *The American Journal of Sports Medicine 7*: 264–7.

Jackson, D. W., et al. "Quadricep Contusions in Young Athletes Relations of Severity of Injury to Treatment and Prognosis." *Journal of Bone and Joint Surgery.* January, 1973, pp. 95–105.

Jackson, Douglas W. "Injury Prediction in the Young Athlete: a Preliminary Report." *The American Journal of Sports Medicine.* January/February, 1978, pp. 6–11.

Jackson; Jarret; Bailey; Kausek; Swanson; and Powel. "Injury Prediction in the Young Athlete: a Preliminary Report." *The American Journal of Sports Medicine 6*(1): 6–14.

James, Stanley; Bates, Barry; and Osternig, Louis. "Injuries to Runners." *The American Journal of Sports Medicine.* March-April, 1978, pp. 40–50.

Jastremski, Chester. "Swimmer's Ear." *Swimming World & Junior Swimmer 19*(9): 98–9.

Jenks, G. "Prevention of Heat Injuries during Distance Running. A Position Statement from the American College of Sports Medicine." *Journal of Sportsmedicine 3*(4): 194–6.

Knight, Kenneth. "Cyrostretch for Muscle Spasm." *The Physician and Sportsmedicine.* April, 1980, pp. 112–8.

Knight, Kenneth. "The Effects of Hypothermia on Inflammation and Swelling." *Athletic Training 11*(1): 7–10.

Knight, Kenneth. "Total Injury Rehabilitation." *The Physician and Sportsmedicine.* August, 1979.

Krauth, B. "Injuries and the Inflammation Process." *Athletic Journal 55:* 94–5.

Krissoff, William B. "Runner's Injuries." *The Physician and Sportsmedicine.* December, 1979, pp. 54–64.

Kuland, Daniel. "Tennis Injuries: Prevention and Treatment, a Review." *The American Journal of Sports Medicine.* July-August, 1979, pp. 249–53.

Landwer, G. E. "Heat." *Runner's World 15*(5): 72–4.

Lestwauik, Joseph J., et al. "Injuries in Interscholastic Wrestling." *The Physician and Sportsmedicine.* March, 1980, p. 111.

Lezberg, Sandra F. "Screening for Scoliosis." *Physical Therapy 54* (4): 371–2.

Mack, William. "Playing Hurt—the Doctor's Dilemma." *Sports Illustrated.* June 11, 1979, pp. 30–6.

McCluskey, George M. "A Treatment for Ankle Sprains." *American Journal of Sports Medicine 4*(4).

Mickelsen, Olaf. "Nutrition and Athletics." *Food and Nutrition News 41*(7): 2–5.

Millar, Anthony. "An Early Stretching Routine for Calf Muscle Strain." *Medicine and Science in Sports.* June, 1976, p. 39.

Mirken, G. "Carbohydrate Loading: a Dangerous Practice." *Journal of the American Medical Association.* March 26, 1973, pp. 1511–2.

94

Mirkin, Kent. "Groin Pain." *The Runner*. April, 1980, p. 12.

Mirtin, Gabe. "Remedies for Shin Splints: What You Can Do to Prevent and Cure Them." *The Runner* 1 (12): 20.

Nelson, Ralph. "What Should Athletes Eat? Un-mixing Folly and Facts." *The Physician and Sportsmedicine*. November, 1975, pp. 67–72.

Nicholas, James. "Injuries to Knee Ligaments." *Journal of the American Medical Association* 212 (13): 2236–9.

Nischl, Robert. "Keeping Fit." *World Tennis*. January, 1979, p. 14.

Olsen, Perry. "How Running Can Hurt Your Back." *The Runner*. April, 1980, p. 61.

Opie, L. H. "Sudden Death and Sport." *Lancet*. February, 1975, pp. 233–6.

Ostrom, Russell C. "Knee Rehabilitation Following Surgical Procedure." *Physical Therapy*. December, 1977, pp. 1376–9.

Pearl, Bill; Kurland, Harvey; Lewis, Mitch; and Wong, Donald. "Injuries: the Agony of Body-building." *Muscle Digest* 4 (1): 17–23.

Pedegana, Larry R. "Waterskiing Injuries." *The Physician and Sportsmedicine*. June, 1979, pp. 108–14.

Pettrone, Frank A. "Acromioclavicular Dislocation." *The American Journal of Sports Medicine*. July-August, 1978, pp. 160–3.

Plowman, S. "Physiological Characteristics of Female Athletes." *Research Quarterly of the AAHPER*. December, 1974, pp. 349–62.

Priest, James; Braden, Vic; and Gerberich, Susan. "The Elbow and Tennis Part I." *The Physician and Sportsmedicine*. April, 1980, pp. 78–86.

Priest, James, and Nagil, Donald. "Tennis Shoulder." *American Journal of Sports Medicine*. January-February, 1976, pp. 28–42.

Priest, James D., et al. "A Study of Players with Pain." *Physician and Sportsmedicine*. May, 1980, pp. 77–85.

Prueske, Eleanor. "The Athletes Foot (Personal Health)." *Current Health* 5 (6): 14–5.

Riley, Dan. "Prevention and Rehabilitation of Injuries." *Scholastic Coach*. March, 1980, 44–6, 96–7.

Shepard, Roy J. "Exercise for the Asthmatic Patient." *Journal of Sports Medicine and Physical Fitness* 18 (3).

Shon, D. H. "Treatment of the Most Common Athletic Injuries." *Athletic Journal* 55: 60.

Sinton, Dr. William A. "The Ankle: Soft Tissue Injuries." *The Journal of Sports Medicine* 1 (3).

Sissel, Bill. "A Fun Way to Develop the Ankle." *Athletic Journal*. February, 1980, pp. 40 and 88.

Smith, J. L., and Bozymowski, M. "Attitude towards Warm-up." *Research Quarterly* 36 (1).

Snedeker, Jeff; Recine, Victor; and MacCarter, Carl. "Cryotherapy and the Athletic Injury." *Athletic Journal* 55: 16+.

Speroff, Leon. "Exercise and Menstrual Function." *The Physician and Sportsmedicine*. May, 1980, pp. 42–52.

Stanitski; McMaster; and Scranton. "On the Nature of Stress Fracture." *The American Journal of Sports Medicine* 6 (6): 391–6.

Starkey, Jerry A. "Treatment of Ankle Sprains by Simultaneous Use of Intermittent Compression and Ice Packs." *The American Journal of Sports Medicine*. July-August, 1976, (4), pp. 142–4.

Subotnick, Steven. "Nine Mistakes Runner's Make." 15 (4).

Tambereli, Al. "Prevention and Care of Knee Injury." *The Athletic Journal*. February, 1978, p. 40.

Torg, J. S., et al. "The National Football Head and Neck Injury Register." *JAMA*. April 6, 1979, pp. 1477–9.

Vincent, L. M. "The War with Water." *Dance Magazine* 53 (7): 96–7.

Walter, Norman E. "Stress Fractures in Young Athletes." *American Journal of Sports Medicine* 5 (4).

Weems, Fred. "What the Coach Should Know about the Pitching Arm." *Scholastic Coach*. April, 1980, pp. 44–7 and 84.

Weiss, D. "Help Prevent Arm Injuries with Stretching Exercises." *Athletic Journal* 57: 50–4.

Wells, Robert L. "Improve Flexibility to Prevent Injuries." *Athletic Journal* 60 (2): 54–5 and 78.

Whiteside, P. A. "Men's and Women's Injuries in Comparable Sports." *Physician and Sportsmedicine* 8 (3): 131–8.

Williams, Melvin. "Drugs and Athletic Performance." 1974, pp. 3–19.

Wilmore, J. H. "Inferiority of Female Athletes: Myth or Reality." *Journal of Sports Medicine* 3 (1): 1–6.

Wynn, Terry. "The Sock Wrap." *The Athletic Journal*. February, 1978, p. 61.

Mouthguards in Athletics

The NAGWS Athletic Training Council strongly endorses the use of mouthguards in athletics. Adopting regulations requiring mouthguards to be worn has resulted in dramatic decreases in mouth, tooth, and head injuries in men's football and ice hockey. Not only do mouthguards provide protection for the teeth, gums, and lips, but they also can be instrumental in absorbing the concussive forces of a blow to the head, neck, or face. The protection a mouthguard provides may be significant enough to prevent and/or to reduce the severity of head injuries in athletics.

Prosthetics and Protective Equipment

Integrating students with handicapping conditions and development of new prosthetic and protective devices, has raised concern among coaches, trainers, and physical educators in regarding the legality of such devices in competitive athletics. If wearing a prosthetic or a protective device enables an individual with a handicapping condition or a previously-injured athlete to compete *safely*, he or she cannot be denied competitive opportunities because such devices are required.

An athlete must first receive medical approval to participate in his or her chosen sport; devices worn must be in accordance with state or local athletic governing body rules and rules of the sport itself. The prosthetic or protective device must pose no hazard to the athlete, his or her teammates, or opponents. Protective devices such as knee braces containing metal parts (including Lenox-Hill knee braces), metal or orthoplast splints, plaster, fiberglass, or silicone (RTV-11) casts, felt, and foam rubber protective padding are all used to protect injured body parts. Such devices should not be allowed if they are dangerous to the athlete, his or her teammates, and opponents. Nor is it acceptable for wearers of prosthetic or protective devices to gain an athletic advantage via the device itself. All such devices must be well-padded so as to avoid presenting a nonyielding or dangerous, harder-than-the-human-body-itself, surface to the individual's teammates or opponents. Most items, when covered with approximately one-half inch of close-cell slow recovery foam rubber, pose no hazard to other participants.

Lacrosse Injuries

Those familiar with the sport of lacrosse remember a day when the men's and women's style of play were entirely different. Traditionally, the men play a hard-hitting, contact game. For them protective gear is both needed and required. In the past, women's lacrosse had been a game of skill, speed, and finesse. Yet now, with women becoming increasingly competitive, the style of play is changing. Injuries, particularly to the head, face, and upper body, have increased as body and stick contact has become more frequent. The option of requiring protective equipment in the women's game is being more frequently discussed.

We, the members of NAGWS Athletic Training Council, feel that the injury situation in women's lacrosse must be closely monitored in future years. We endorse the following:

1. Upgrade the quality of coaching and officiating by more frequent and more comprehensive clinics and instructional sessions offered by NAGWS/ USWLA. Included should be informa-

tion concerning proper conditioning, correct skill execution, safe playing areas and equipment, rules interpretations, etc.

2. Provide for stricter rule enforcement of existing rules, including the use of yellow (warning) and red (suspension) cards for dangerous checking, barricading, and face-checking. Offending players and their teams *must* be responsible for their dangerous actions.

3. Consider rule changes to reduce potentially injurious situations from developing, i.e., stricter and more explicit wording of rules concerning stick-checking, face-checking, and barricading, etc.

4. Carefully monitor injury statistics via NAIRS and surveys of individual institution injury records through NATA-certified trainers.

5. An effort should be made on the part of players, coaches, trainers, fans, and athletic administrators to maintain the beauty and integrity of women's lacrosse.

6. Mouthguards should be worn to reduce or prevent the incidence of injury to teeth, gums, mouth, etc.

Suggested Preparation for Emergency Situations during Practice and Competition

Equipment that should be *readily accessible* in a nearby training room or storage room for all practices and games in field hockey, volleyball, basketball, gymnastics, softball, swimming and diving, and track and field is listed below:

- stretcher;
- spine board*(short) with neck traction unit (if unit is unavailable, substitute 4 five-pound sandbags);
- blanket;
- crutches;
- cervical collar;
- arm sling (a large muslin triangular bandage with two safety pins may be substituted).

Equipment that should be readily available on the field or court for all practices and games in any sport is listed below:

- splints—board, plastic air, cardboard, or ladder;
- ice with small plastic bags;
- towels;
- elastic wraps—3", 4", 6";
- water—drinking fountain, cooler, hose, plastic squirt bottles;

- first aid kit.

Items suggested for the first aid kit:

- variety of tape;
- tape adherent;
- tape remover;
- underwrap;
- tape cutter;
- bandage scissors;
- nail clippers;
- tweezers;
- pen light;
- cleansing agent;
- alcohol or substitute;
- Hydrogen Peroxide;
- first aid cream;
- petroleum jelly (Vaseline);
- sterile gauze pads—3" × 3", 4" × 4";
- band aids 1-3, ¾" × 3", extra large;
- gauze rolls—2";
- analgesic—mild;
- gauze sponges—3" × 3";
- tongue depressors;
- cotton-tipped applicators;
- ammonia capsules;
- hand mirror;
- ophthalmolic solution — sterile;
- contact lense wetting solution—sterile;
- combine;
- felt;
- foam—¼", ⅜";
- elastic wraps—4";
- safety pins;
- rubberbands;
- needle and thread;
- tampons;
- aspirin.**

In addition, the trainer or coach covering a sport should:

1. Know where the nearest phone is located.
2. Have $.20 taped to the first aid kit for use in a pay phone.
3. Carry a first aid emergency care manual.
4. Know procedure for securing ambulance service.
5. Post all emergency phone numbers, including the team physician's on the inside of the first aid kit and adjacent to the phone in the training room and/or office.
6. Carry the telephone numbers of each athlete's parents or guardian if working with minors.

---

*Only to be used by trained medical or paramedical personnel.
**Ability to dispense medication, including aspirin, may be prohibited by school regulations.

Appendix C
Recommended Readings

Albohm, Marge. *Health Care for the Female Athlete.* Florida: The Athletic Institute, 1982.

American Alliance for Health, Physical Education, Recreation and Dance. *Youth Sports Guide—for Coaches and Parents.* Washington, DC: The American Alliance for Health, Physical Education, Recreation and Dance, 1977.

American Red Cross. *Advanced First Aid and Emergency Care.* Garden City, NY: Doubleday and Company, Inc., 1979.

Anderson, Bob. *Stretching.* Palmer Lake, CO: Stretching Inc., 1975.

Consumers Union. *The Medicine Show.* New York: Pantheon Books, 1976.

Cooper, Kenneth. *The Aerobics Way.* New York: Bantam Books, 1977.

Fox, Edward, and Mathews, Donald. *Interval Training.* Philadelphia, PA: W. B. Saunders Company, 1974.

Galton, Lawrence. *Your Child in Sports.* New York: Franklin Watts, 1980.

Haycock, Christine, ed. *Sports Medicine for the Athletic Female.* Oradell, NJ: Medical Economics, 1978.

Henderson, John. *Emergency Medical Guide.* New York: McGraw-Hill Book Company, 1978.

Jackson, Douglas, and Pescar, Susan. *The Young Athlete's Health Handbook.* New York: Everest House Publishers, 1981.

Kapit, Wynn, and Elson, Lawrence. *The Anatomy Coloring Book.* New York: A Canfield Press/ Barnes and Noble Book, 1977.

Klafs, Carl, and Arnheim, Daniel. *Modern Principles of Athletic Training.* St. Louis, MO: C. V. Mosby Company, 1981.

Klafs, Carl, and Lyon, M. Joan. *The Female Athlete.* St. Louis, MO: C. V. Mosby Company, 1978.

Marshall, John, with Barbash, Heather. *The Sports Doctor's Fitness Book for Women.* New York: Dell Publishing Company, 1981.

The Physician and Sportsmedicine, Suite 200, 4530 West 77th St., Minneapolis, MN 55435.

Smith, Nathan. *Food for Sport.* Palo Alto, CA: Bull Publishing Company, 1976.

Southmayd, William, and Hoffman, Marshall. *Sportshealth.* New York: Quick Fox, 1981.

The National Association for Girls and Women in Sport
an association of
The American Alliance for Health, Physical Education, Recreation and Dance
1900 Association Drive, Reston, Virginia 22091

ISBN 0-88314-231-7